YORK NOTES

General Editors: Professor A.N. J̶̶̶
of Stirling) & Professor Suheil Bus̶̶
University of Beirut)

G000061103

H.G.Wells

THE HISTORY OF MR POLLY

Notes by Martin Stephen

BA (LEEDS) PH D (SHEFFIELD)
Second Master,
Sedbergh School

LONGMAN
YORK PRESS

Extracts from *The History of Mr Polly* are reprinted by
kind permission of the estate of H.G. Wells.

YORK PRESS
Immeuble Esseily, Place Riad Solh, Beirut.

LONGMAN GROUP LIMITED
Longman House, Burnt Mill, Harlow,
Essex CM20 2JE, England
and Associated Companies throughout the world.

First published 1980
Reprinted 1984
ISBN 0 582 78132 9
Printed in Hong Kong by
Sheck Wah Tong Printing Press Ltd

Contents

Part 1

Introduction

The life of H.G. Wells

Herbert George Wells was born on 21 September 1866, above a small china and hardware shop which his parents owned in Bromley, Kent, one of England's southern counties. He was the youngest of four children, and there was nothing in his birth or background to suggest that he would in time become one of the world's most famous writers and thinkers, a man whose novels, short stories, historical, scientific, and sociological books would sell millions of copies.

His parents had been domestic servants in a Victorian country house, but had left there and invested their savings in the Bromley shop. The business appears to have been permanently on the brink of bankruptcy, and Mr Wells had to supplement the family income by playing cricket professionally. He was an excellent cricketer, playing for the Kent county team, and his visits away to play the sport, although justified on financial grounds, must have provided a welcome relief from the boredom and worry of his life as a small shopkeeper. However, the family was not an unhappy one, at least in the early days, and Mr Wells was able to stimulate his son's interest in literature by bringing home books for him to read from the Bromley lending library. Despite this, Wells appears to have felt closer to his mother than he did to his father.

Wells attended two schools when he was young, but both appear to have been depressing and educationally very unsatisfactory institutions, and he continued to obtain what he saw as his real education from the lending library. However good or bad it may have been, his education ceased suddenly when his father suffered a bad fall, and had to give up the shop. The family could no longer afford to pay for Herbert's schooling, and it became an urgent requirement that he should start to earn his own living. Before he was fourteen he found himself apprenticed to Messrs Rogers and Denyer, a firm of drapers (dealers in cloth and clothing) in Windsor. It was a disaster. His employers found him inattentive, uncivil, dreamy, uninterested, and also unable to give customers the correct change, and within two months he was on his way home again.

Meanwhile, his mother had returned to Up Park in Sussex, the country house where she had been employed before the move into the china shop, and was now housekeeper to Miss Fetherstonhaugh, the owner. Mrs Wells had a distant cousin ('Uncle Williams') who had recently become headmaster of a small National School in Wookey, Somerset, and before long Herbert was installed there as a pupil teacher. This arrangement, quite common at the time, meant that in return for undertaking simple teaching duties he would be fed, given a room, and helped to continue his own studies. However, headmaster and pupil lost their jobs after three months, when it was proved that Uncle Williams had forged references in order to obtain the post. Herbert was back with his mother for the Christmas holiday of 1879.

After a short while he found himself in the town of Midhurst, apprenticed to a chemist. He quite enjoyed this, especially as it meant that he had to attend some lessons at Midhurst Grammar School in order to learn Latin, which he needed if he was to understand and label the various substances used by the chemist. However, it soon became clear that more money than was available would be needed if he was to qualify as a chemist, and he was forced to end his apprenticeship. There were further problems; Mrs Wells was proving an inefficient house-keeper, and to avoid the embarrassment of having her son return to Up Park for the third time within a year, she agreed to his boarding for six weeks at Midhurst Grammar School, where he impressed the head-master with his enthusiasm and willingness to learn.

Herbert's brief period of happiness was destined to be short. In desperation, he was yet again apprenticed to a draper, the choice this time falling on Hyde's Drapery Stores, Southsea. It may seem strange that his mother sent him yet again to a drapery firm, but she was becoming desperate to secure his future, and all the other forms of employment that he thought he might like were more expensive than his mother could afford. All apprenticeships had to be paid for by the apprentice himself, or by his parents or guardian. He started work in Southsea in May 1880, and the two years that followed were among the most miserable of his whole life. It was not only that he had to live in dormitories and cold rooms, working long hours at a job he hated, in return for poor food and wages; his brief time at Midhurst had also shown him the pleasures of learning, and that he could learn quickly, and this must have increased his feelings that he was wasting his life, and doomed never to do that at which he was happiest. 'I stuck that hell of a life', he wrote, 'for two years to August, 1882 . . . I ran away one Sunday morning to my mother, and told her that I would rather die than go on being a draper. That seventeen-mile tramp, without break-fast, to deliver that ultimatum is still very vivid in my memory.' Hungry, weary, and in the last stages of desperation, he met his mother on her way home from church, and threatened to commit suicide unless his agreement with the drapers' firm was cancelled. Unwillingly, his mother agreed.

It was then that his future took a turn for the better. Writing to Mr Bryatt, the headmaster of Midhurst Grammar School, he was taken on at sixteen years of age as a teacher, at a salary of £20 per annum. Although he bitterly resented having to be confirmed into the Church of England as a condition of being employed by the school, he worked hard enough in his year at Midhurst to win a scholarship of a guinea (£1.05) a week to the Normal School of Science in South Kensington, London; this is now the Royal College of Science. For his first year all went well, especially as his biology professor was the inspiring scholar and thinker T.H. Huxley. As time went on, however, his academic performance declined, as he started to read more and more literature, and eventually he failed his degree examination. Although he later gained his degree, his initial failure meant that he was poorly qualified, and that he had to accept a teaching position in a rather second-rate private school at Holt, near Wrexham. Whilst refereeing a football match he was severely kicked, perhaps intentionally, and ruptured a kidney. He later had a lung haemorrhage, and might well have died had not the long-suffering Miss Fetherstonhaugh of Up Park agreed to his being taken in and cared for in the house for three months. This was the start of the ill-health which affected him for the rest of his life.

In 1887 he returned to London with five pounds in his pocket and with some idea of being a writer. The next few years were very busy ones for him. He taught in a number of schools, and in his spare time studied for his B.Sc. as an external student at London University; in later years this same university was to award him the honorary degree of Doctor of Literature. He obtained his B.Sc. in 1888. In 1891, he fell in love with and married his cousin Isabella. The marriage was a failure, and he left Isabella in 1894, divorced her, and married Amy Catherine Robbins, who had once been one of his students. This second marriage was to last until Amy's death in 1927, and gave Wells much-needed stability and security. Amy adored her husband, and remained faithful to him throughout her life, despite his string of mistresses and volatile temperament.

The event which was to change his life must have seemed an absolute disaster when it first happened. He burst a blood vessel in his lungs, had to give up teaching, and spent three months convalescing at Eastbourne in southern England. In desperation, and in order to earn some money, he began to write magazine articles, an area in which he had already had some small experience. The articles were a success, and he was set on his way to becoming a full-time writer. He published his first book, *A Textbook of Biology*, in 1893, and followed this in 1895 with his first major novel, *The Time Machine*. In the years that followed he wrote many more books, up to four a year, and also found time to stand as a Socialist candidate for Parliament in 1922 and 1923, although on neither occasion was he elected. He died in 1946, aged eighty, depressed by the turn that world events had taken, but still writing, and still commanding attention whenever he did so.

Wells and *The History of Mr Polly*

It is obvious that there are many links that can be drawn between Wells's own life and the events and characters of *The History of Mr Polly*. Sometimes these can be found in the smallest of details, as when Rumbold, the china-dealer, unpacks his cases with his back to the wind, so that the straw does not blow into his eyes. Mr Polly must surely owe this description to the young H.G. Wells, who must have helped his father unpack such cases, with their straw padding, on numerous occasions. Of course, the links go much deeper than this. The whole background of poor shopkeepers struggling to earn a living in the book is drawn from Wells's own childhood experiences. Mr Polly's buying of job-lots of books is exactly what Wells's father did, and the account of what the young Mr Polly read follows pretty exactly Wells's own tastes and experience, even to the dislike of Sir Walter Scott. Mr Polly's confused reaction to the death of his father probably reflects much of what Wells himself thought when his own father died. The attack on education in *The History of Mr Polly* reflects Wells's disgust at his own schooling, even to the criticism of National Schools. The satire of the church found in the description of Mr Polly's marriage can be linked with the outrage that Wells felt when forced to join the Church of England in order to be able to teach. There is even a physical likeness between the two, for Wells was a short, tubby man; like Mr Polly, Wells also had trouble in his youth with careless and wayward speech, using many of the words that he had read in books, but never heard properly pronounced. Perhaps the most obvious links of all are those centred round the drapery business, the main difference being that in *The History of Mr Polly* it is Parsons who 'gets out' of the business in dramatic style, and not Polly.

All these links, and many more, make it very easy to see Mr Polly as simply a fictional version of Wells himself. This idea needs to be treated with great caution. Certainly there are elements of autobiography in *The History of Mr Polly*, and much of the time Wells is undoubtedly writing from within his own experience, but there is much that is left out. Mr Polly does not suffer severe illness, study for a university degree, teach, or become in any way connected with the life of a great country house, as Wells certainly was. It is true that both Wells and Polly have unhappy first marriages to cousins, but the similarity stops there; the marriages ended very differently. Wells would certainly never have been content with the post of ferryman at a country inn, and there is nothing in Mr Polly of the gnawing, almost ruthless ambition that typified Wells. Nor was Wells anything like the comical, self-defeating character that we see in Mr Polly; very few people who met Wells failed to take him seriously. Mr Polly is therefore firmly a fictional character, albeit one who benefits from Wells's own experience and insight. To see this any other way harms one of the central features of the book, that in which the reader is asked to see Mr Polly as a representative figure. His problems of middle age, an unhappy marriage, and dissatisfaction with his way of life are universal and shared by many people, and Wells intends everyone to see something of himself in Mr Polly. Only if the reader does this can he get the full flavour and significance of the novel, and to identify Mr Polly too closely with the character of Wells destroys this aim, by limiting it.

The work of H.G. Wells

By the time he died, Wells had written over one hundred books, as well as numerous short stories, radio plays, pamphlets, and film scripts. His novels divide themselves into roughly three groupings.

The first, and possibly still the best known, is that of his 'fantasy' novels, which would be described nowadays as science fiction; the most famous are probably *The Time Machine* (1895), *The Invisible Man* (1897), *The War of the Worlds* (1898), *The First Men in the Moon* (1901), and *The War in the Air* (1908), although this is by no means a complete list. These were the novels that established his fame as a writer, and what he did in them was to use his knowledge of science to prophesy how society would develop in the future. Although Wells insisted that these novels were political in their nature, they do not examine either politics or the structure of society in any great depth, and it was the science and spectacular prophecies in these novels that caught and held the popular imagination. Today academic critics tend to dismiss the early novels, and it is true that things that were daring prophecies in the 1890s, such as air warfare and improved methods of transport, have become so common as to arouse no special interest. In other areas, too, the books can appear dated; now that we have landed men on the moon, Wells's ideas about how it would be done appear clumsy, indeed quite plainly wrong. On the other hand, these books are still widely read, and have inspired modern writers to adapt them into television, radio, and film scripts.

Increasingly, Wells's reputation is coming to be based on the novels that he wrote in the middle of his career (very roughly, between 1905 and 1918). In these novels science is dropped in favour of looking at people, and in particular the attempts of the lower middle classes in England to better themselves. *Kipps* (1905) and *The History of Mr Polly*

(1910) are generally considered to be the best of this group, and *Tono-Bungay* (1909) is still widely read and admired. These novels specialise in vivid characterisation and in the examination of lower middle-class society.

In his last years, Wells turned increasingly to novels of ideas, in which fiction was all but dropped, and he discussed openly his views on world society and human nature. He also wrote an immensely successful *Short History of the World* (1922).

The literary and historical background

In 1866, when Wells was born, most of Europe had hardly come to terms with the steam railway engine; in 1946, when he died, mankind had exploded the first atom bomb. Such was the vastness of the changes that came about during his lifetime.

The major event of the years prior to Wells's birth had been the Industrial Revolution, that process by which Great Britain turned itself from an agricultural nation to one almost wholly dependent on industry for its wealth and prosperity. Although the economy had changed, many areas of society had not. The population had soared, and vast teeming cities sprung up where before there had only been villages; by 1870, over two-thirds of the population were urban dwellers. One of the results of this was a tendency to romanticise the country and look back to the imaginary 'good times' in the villages of rural England, where the sun always shone, there was food and beer in plenty, and everyone was happy. The image was false, of course (the country could be as hard and cruel as the town, as can be seen in novels like Thomas Hardy's *Tess of the d'Urbervilles* (1891) or W.H. Davies's *Autobiography of a Super-tramp* (1907), and living conditions may even have been better for the urban working man than they were for the farm labourer, but this did not stop people dreaming. One of the complaints levelled against *The History of Mr Polly* is that the vision of the countryside contained in it is unreal and idealised, a city dweller's vision of what the countryside should be like.

Another result of the industrialisation of England was the creation of whole new classes of people; skilled and unskilled workers, low-grade clerks, shopkeepers, domestic servants, all these groups grew in increasing numbers to feed the demands of industry and the new wealth it created. Lacking any deep-rooted culture of their own, these classes adopted the middle-class virtues of hard work and sober living, but often found them incapable of meeting the demands of the new society. This swirling mass of people, unhappy without being able to see the cause of their unhappiness or affect it in any way, appear in many late-Victorian novels, including, of course, *The History of Mr Polly*. In this novel, Mr Rusper is bravely trying to understand a pamphlet about tariff reform, but as soon as he sees the fire that is about to consume his shop, he 'ceased to believe the Fiscal Question the most urgent of human affairs'. It is obvious that Rusper cannot control or understand his own future, never mind that of his country, and there is sad irony in his jotting down the figure of twelve million pounds in the margin of his pamphlet when his own shop is facing bankruptcy for the want of a few pounds. It was not until after the First World War that people such as Rusper and Mr Polly were able to benefit from improved education and have more control over the way their country was run.

In the year that *The History of Mr Polly* was published, literature was also in a state of change. The great Victorian writers were mostly dead (Charles Dickens died in 1870, Alfred Lord Tennyson in 1892, George Eliot in 1880), and many of the new wave of authors (T.S. Eliot, Virginia Woolf, James Joyce) did not become widely known until the 1920s. Also changing was the idea that the novel should be read by a wide range of people, from servants to lords, but this did not greatly affect Wells, who demanded and expected a wide readership for his books, and judged their success on the basis of how many copies they had sold.

Science and industry had brought many advantages to the society in which H.G. Wells lived, but also many problems. *The History of Mr Polly* looks at some of these problems, but is never defeated by them; it is Wells's own statement that, however complex society may become, the human individual will always be able to establish his own identity within it if he is prepared, like Mr Polly, to take the risks.

A note on the text

There are no textual problems with *The History of Mr Polly*; there are several modern editions, nearly all of which use as their base the text given in the Atlantic Edition of Wells's work, published by Macmillan, London, in twenty-eight volumes, between 1924 and 1927. These have a preface by Wells.

For the majority of students, a perfectly satisfactory text can be found in that published by Pan Books, London, 1963.

Part 2

Summaries
of THE HISTORY OF MR POLLY

A general summary

Mr Polly hates the town of Fishbourne, the small draper's shop that he owns in it, his wife, his neighbours, and, most of all, he hates himself for having led a life that after thirty-seven years has given him nothing but worry, frustration, and boredom. His little shop is facing bankruptcy, and everything seems hopeless.

His education taught him very little, and confused him horribly about the things he did know, but even this ended when he was fourteen and sent as apprentice to a firm of drapers. Although he dislikes his job, he meets two other men at the drapery store, Parsons and Platt, and as the 'three P's' they spend many 'jolly days of companionship' together. But Parsons is dismissed, and it is never the same again for Mr Polly. He leaves, and takes up a succession of jobs that get steadily worse as he increasingly loses any enthusiasm for the work he does.

Suddenly, his father dies, and at the funeral Mr Polly learns that he has been left three hundred and ninety-five pounds by his father. He also meets three girl cousins for the first time. He takes a short holiday, and has a short, sad romance with a schoolgirl, but finds himself drawn back more and more often to his cousins. They want husbands, he wants warmth and companionship to replace that which he had with Parsons and Platt. Almost by accident, Mr Polly proposes to his cousin Miriam, and before he can withdraw, Mr Polly finds himself married and running a small drapery shop in Fishbourne, a seaside town. His marriage is a disaster, and he soon comes to hate all that is around and within him. This is how we find him at the start of the book.

He decides to kill himself, and works out a complex plan to burn down the shop and slit his own throat; if this is done carefully, Miriam will get the insurance money on the shop and on Mr Polly's life, and he will not have her on his conscience. But the plan goes wrong, and Mr Polly becomes a hero, rescuing an old lady and delighting the owners of the shops burnt down in the fire, who would rather have the insurance money than they would the buildings.

Made bold by his success, Mr Polly leaves Miriam, and wanders happily through the countryside. The landlady of the Potwell Inn offers him a job as ferryman and general help. He accepts with delight, not realising that 'Uncle' Jim, the landlady's nephew, is terrorising her and threatening violence to any man who tries to help her. After much worrying Mr Polly decides to fight it out with Jim, and in a series of encounters succeeds in driving him off, although his victory is gained more through luck than by any skill as a fighter. In the final battle, Jim steals Mr Polly's clothes.

After five years, Mr Polly's conscience troubles him, and he returns to Fishbourne to see Miriam. She has set up a tea-shop with the proceeds of Mr Polly's life insurance, which was paid to her when Jim's dead body was mistakenly identified as that of Mr Polly by the clothes that were on it. Mr Polly, his conscience at ease, returns happily to the Potwell Inn.

Detailed summaries

Chapter 1: Beginnings, and the Bazaar

Mr Polly is sitting on a stile, between two 'threadbare-looking' fields, suffering from acute indigestion and a strong feeling that the world is a 'beastly' place. He has had an argument with his wife and stormed out for a walk to try and cheer himself up, but it is a losing battle. He hates his wife, his shop, the town of Fishbourne, and all his neighbours, and 'with indescribable bitterness he hated himself' for having let himself get into a 'silly Hole' where everything he does seems fated to be miserable and depressing. Matters are not helped by his indigestion, caused in this case by his wife's bad cooking and his own liking for mixed pickles.

After being loved and adored as a baby, Mr Polly's mother died when he was seven, and he was sent first to a National School, and then a small private school. These 'dingy' places left him bored and confused, unable at fourteen years of age to spell or pronounce words correctly, or to do basic arithmetic. The only thing which kept his spirits up during this battering was reading, and this gave him hope that romance, excitement, and adventure did exist in the world, somewhere.

At fourteen, he was apprenticed to the Port Burdock Drapery Bazaar. Most of the time, he was 'inattentive to business', but lived 'in a sort of uncomfortable happiness'. The happiness came from the stirrings of interest he began to feel with regard to girls, and the companionship of Platt and Parsons, two other apprentices. These three called themselves the 'three P's', and they spent many happy hours together, going for long walks, going into pubs (places where alcoholic drinks can be purchased and consumed) when they could afford it, and getting Parsons, who read everything he could lay his hands on, to recite aloud passages from the books he was reading. As for Mr Polly, he was attracted by any new word or striking phrase, but because of his poor education, often did not know how to spell or pronounce these. His solution to his problem was to pronounce them so badly that people would think it was done on purpose, and not through ignorance.

COMMENTARY: Wells starts his novel in the middle of the story, and then goes back to the beginning of Mr Polly's life. This is a more dramatic and interesting way of starting, but it may confuse the reader.

Notice how quickly Wells gets his characters speaking, and how much we learn about them from the manner in which they speak. Notice also how Wells emphasises a point or mood by repeating words and phrases: for instance, he gives us 'Hole', 'Hat!', and five repetitions of 'hated' in one short paragraph. Wells also uses the word 'cold' three times in describing the meal Mr Polly has just had. As well as suggesting that the meal was unappetising, this also gives an impression of the atmosphere in the house when the meal was being eaten.

The short but accurate physical descriptions of characters that we find in this first chapter are typical of Wells's style, as is his description of Mr Polly's indigestion; talking about this as if it were on the same level as an epic and heroic struggle, or a revolution, makes the indigestion appear comic and slightly ridiculous.

The first chapter establishes the character of Mr Polly as that of a romantic dreamer whose life seems always destined never to live up to his dreams. He is an amusing character, towards whom we feel some sympathy, but he is also rather pathetic; he seems to lack the skill and determination necessary to improve his life. This chapter also introduces some of the book's themes, notably the ineffectual worrying of the lower middle classes, the harm done to a child's imagination by the English educational system, the misery of the apprentice system (especially when in conjunction with the drapery business), the joy of friendship, the beauty of the English countryside, the misery of religion and religious people, and the horror of a bad marriage. We also learn that through reading a person can enter a world of beauty and romance, where the troubles of everyday life can be temporarily forgotten. The tone of the book (comic, but with serious undertones) is also established.

NOTES AND GLOSSARY:
Words or phrases which can be found in any good dictionary of English are not glossed.

Laocoon struggle: in Greek mythology Laocoon was a Trojan soldier who struggled heroically against two serpents who crushed both him and his two sons

Marseillaise: a famous French song, now that country's national anthem, and associated with the French Revolution

tumbrils: carts used for carrying people to the guillotine in the French Revolution

desgenerated: Mr Polly's version of 'degenerate'

localized embonpoint: a fat stomach

First the infant ... arms: from Jaques's seven ages of man speech in Shakespeare's *As You Like It*

National School: a school run by the National Society, a private body

Catechism: a set of questions and answers that have to be learnt by anyone wishing to be confirmed into the Church of England

Revivalist week: the time when a travelling evangelical preacher visited an area, stirring up a frenzy of religious observance

dratted: a term of abuse

diurnal: daily

demi-monde: women on the outskirts of society with bad reputations for immorality

au courant: in touch with affairs

Romeo and Juliet ... **'We bite our Thumbs':** *Romeo and Juliet* is an early play by Shakespeare, set in Verona, about the tragic love of two people. The lines about biting thumbs are spoken early in the play, and refer to the fact that to do this to somebody was an insult in Shakespeare's time

Bocashieu: Boccaccio (1313–75), famous Italian author

amours: (*French*) love-affairs

Rabooloose: Rabelais (1495–1553), great French writer

Gargantua: a giant with a vast appetite featured in one of Rabelais' works

YMCA: Young Men's Christian Association, an organisation known largely for the hostels for young people that it runs in major cities

Joy de Vive: for (*French*) 'joie de vivre', the joy of living

ironclads: battleships

argy bargy: noisy argument

salitas: small hills

Sesquippledan verboojuice: sesquipedalian means a foot and a half long: when applied to words it means long and pedantic. Presumably verboojuice means verbiage, wordy stuff, a pompous array of words: so the two words reinforce each other

Eloquent Rapsodooce: eloquent rhapsody

Spuming! Windmilling!: reading in a dramatic manner

articulariously: version of articulate?

Chapter 2: The Dismissal of Parsons

'Suddenly Parsons got himself dismissed.' As far as Parsons is concerned, the art of window dressing (laying goods out for display in shop windows) is in its infancy, and held back by ideas that are too formal, conventional, and restricting. Parsons is going to alter this, and show what can be done.

On the day that Parsons is to dress his window, Mr Polly and Platt cannot restrain their excitement. They continually go out into the street to see Parsons working excitedly on his window, filling it with colour and exciting disarray. But Mr Garvace, the man in charge of the store, is horrified at what Parsons has done. He instructs Morrison, another window dresser, to re-do the window. When Morrison tries to do so, Parsons attacks him with a roll of cloth, and then hits Mr Garvace over his bald head. There is chaos, with cloth and goods flying everywhere, until Parsons is finally overpowered. As well as being dismissed from his job, Parsons is tried in court for assault. After the trial, in which no serious action is taken against Parsons, Mr Polly returns to the dormitory, to find that all trace of Parsons has vanished. Mr Polly is in tears.

COMMENTARY: Parsons's actions show how futile it is to try to fight against society, or hope that it will allow one any individuality. His action in fighting Mr Garvace is like Mr Polly's arson later on in the book, a bid for freedom, but where Mr Polly succeeds, Parsons fails, and has nothing to show for his bid except ruin. Parsons's action is a dream come true for Mr Polly and all the apprentices who had wanted to hit Mr Garvace, but the cold practicality of the policeman and the harsh reality of the law court show how unrealistic and dangerous such dreams can be. We are reminded also by Parsons of how difficult it is to get jobs, something that will later come to affect Mr Polly as well. Parsons's departure leaves Mr Polly in tears, and shows how important this companionship had been to him.

NOTES AND GLOSSARY:

Improver:	someone who has finished his apprenticeship, and is working for low wages in order to gain experience
Manchester department:	a department that sells cotton goods, so called because these were often made in Manchester
Heavy:	a powerful mood
Rockcockyo:	rococo, a very heavily decorated style of architecture
bar sinister:	a term taken from heraldry, suggesting a diagonal strip of material across the window
Egrugious:	possibly egregious, but probably meaningless

Lill dog:	means little dog; another meaningless phrase, but used by Mr Polly when he wants to get out of an awkward situation
silesia:	thin cloth
Allittritions:	Mr Polly's version of alliteration
Bolton sheeting:	sheet material made in Bolton, in Lancashire, England
huckaback:	rough linen cloth
Humbug:	fool; a term of abuse
swapped:	dismissed
perjoocery:	perjury
Bench:	collective noun meaning a number of magistrates sitting in judgment
altaclation:	altercation, argument
crib:	job
refs:	references
Boko:	nose
choleraic:	choleric, angry, hot-tempered
bound over:	not punished, as long as he got into no more trouble
Piping my Eye:	crying, weeping

Chapter 3: Cribs

Port Burdock becomes a depressing place for Mr Polly after Parsons leaves; in his letters, Parsons shows an interest in Socialism, and appears to be a different person from the one Mr Polly used to know. Without Parsons, Platt becomes 'a tiresome companion'. Mr Polly leaves Port Burdock, and has to wait two months before he can find another job. For two weeks he lives in a house belonging to a married cousin in Easewood, where his ailing father is also staying; but Polly is not welcome, and he moves into a hostel. He finds looking for jobs immensely depressing, and the other people who are doing the same thing even more so.

Mr Polly drifts through various jobs, losing interest (and jobs) more and more as time goes on. He goes to a job in Canterbury, which impresses him with its architecture and atmosphere; there he sees and is presses him with its architecture and atmosphere; there he sees and is im-one night. He finds a new job in a dingy London shop, but is accused of lacking energy and enthusiasm, and becomes increasingly miserable.

COMMENTARY: In this chapter there is one of the most significant images in the whole novel, that in which Mr Polly is described as being like a rabbit in a net, trapped and helpless. This description not only applies to Mr Polly, but also to all the people of his class.

This chapter also marks the start of Mr Polly's real unhappiness. It is the time that 'It was brought home to him not so much vividly as with a harsh ungainly insistence that he was a failure in his trade.' Not much is added to the plot in this chapter, but the lengthy descriptions of the drapery trade and the people in it explain Mr Polly's misery, and show what a dreary and unsatisfying way of life it is. It shows us even more strongly that Mr Polly has imagination and a taste for beauty that his way of life cannot satisfy. Though the reader can see this, Mr Polly cannot, and his depression is all the more heavy because he can see no way of removing it, or really understand what it is he wants from life. The Americans symbolise a more forceful and exciting way of life that is truly foreign to people of Mr Polly's class.

The glossary gives the words that Mr Polly is probably aiming for in his mispronunciations. To avoid confusion, notice that even in their proper form the words may not mean anything. We know that Mr Polly means 'lunatic' when he says 'lune-attic' (he knows that *lune* means 'moon' in Latin, and uses the word because the moon influences tides, and it is the tide that kept him out late), but in the context in which he uses it, 'lunatic' and 'lune-attic' are equally nonsensical.

NOTES AND GLOSSARY:

society women: upper-class women

Exorbiant Largenial: for exuberant laryngeal, meaning energetic larynx, a loud talker

Loogoobuosity: for lugubriousness, sadness

Shoveacious: people who push a lot to get their own way

Dejuiced: people with all the spirit taken out of them

Chubby Chops: someone who is fat around the mouth and jaws

Excelsior: (*Latin*, meaning higher). Used here in the sense of the best; also name of a poem by Longfellow (1807–82), an American poet

Baptist: a member of the Baptist Church, Protestant Christian Church

Obsequies: for obsequious, servile, abject, cringing

Stertoraneous: for stertorous; snorting

ex-President Roosevelt: Theodore Roosevelt (1858–1910), President of the USA 1901–9. He, like Baden-Powell, Peter Keary and Samuel Smiles, had a name for being able to inspire enthusiasm for his beliefs

General Baden-Powell: Baden-Powell (1857–1941) was the famous defender of Mafeking for the British in the Boer War, and founder of the Boy Scout movement

Mr Peter Keary: Keary (1865–1915) was a writer and magazine editor, well-known in Mr Polly's day

Dr Samuel Smiles: Smiles (1812–1904) was a surgeon, and author of a famous book, *Self-Help* (1859)

Mr St Loe Strachey: editor and writer (1860–1927)

Falstaff: comic character from Shakespeare's plays *Henry IV*, Parts I & II, and *The Merry Wives of Windsor*

Hudibras: main character in Samuel Butler's *Hudibras*, satirical poem published in 1664; used here as an example of a larger-than-life comic character

Washington Irving: Irving (1783–1859) was a popular American writer who came to live in England

Canterbury: one of England's most beautiful cathedral cities

Gothic architecture: style of architecture popular in England from the twelfth to the sixteenth century

capons: for canons

metrorious urnfuls: for meritorious, praiseworthy, urns

funererial: for funereal

'Canterbury Tales': *The Canterbury Tales* were a group of stories written by Geoffrey Chaucer (1340?–1400), a medieval author and courtier, and were supposedly told by pilgrims on their way to Canterbury

wife of Bath: a large and much-married woman who tells one of the stories in *The Canterbury Tales*

Chaucer's 'Chequers': an inn mentioned by Chaucer

Rapacacity: for rapacity, great greed, avarice

Vorocious: for voracious

Marlowe monument: Christopher Marlowe (1564–93), a great Elizabethan author and dramatist, born in Canterbury

Praposition: proposition; Wells is attempting to imitate an American accent

hustle: hurry; American slang

lune-attic: for lunatic, mad

driving establishment: a shop where the assistants were driven to work very hard

Nar: mispronunciation of 'now'

Vim: slang word, meaning energy, enthusiasm

slacker: someone who does not work hard

buck up: get a move on, work harder

pince-nez: a pair of spectacles with nothing at the side, kept on the face by clipping to the nose

---

Chapter 4: Mr Polly an Orphan

Mr Polly's father dies suddenly. Mr Polly is shocked, uncertain about what to do, and feels guilty that he had not seen his father more. However, his cousins, the Johnsons, take over arrangements for the funeral, and Mr Polly is left to ponder the fact that his father left him three hundred and fifty-five pounds in insurance money. Cousin Johnson has a great deal of advice for Mr Polly on how he should spend the money, including the suggestion that he might rent or buy a small shop.

At the funeral, Mr Polly meets three girl cousins, the Larkins sisters, for the first time, and their large and demonstrative mother. They are very friendly towards him, and he also meets Uncle Pentstemon, a mean, miserly, aggressive old man. Alone of the mourners, Mr Polly feels sad at his father's death; for the others, the funeral is almost 'an enjoyable experience'.

COMMENTARY: Mr Polly is shocked by his father's death; although he hardly knew him as a person, it makes Mr Polly feel even more lonely and isolated. The 'weakly wilful being, struggling to get obdurate things round impossible corners' sums up Mr Polly, his father, and all the people caught in the net of life who feel they are helpless and powerless to do what they want.

The Johnsons and the guests at the funeral see it as a social event, and think little about the dead man: 'She made dying seem almost agreeable.' We are reminded again of how impractical Mr Polly is, when Mrs Johnson has to do all the organising for the funeral. Johnson is shown as a happier version of Mr Polly, an immensely well-meaning man who is also totally boring, and lacks the imagination and aspirations of Mr Polly. His cousins are 'easy people to get along with', and Mr Polly so needs warmth and friendship that he is blinded to their limitations. Uncle Pentstemon is not so blinded; unpleasant though he is, he also acts as a voice of truth.

Wells has a superb ability to write amusing dialogue that tells us a great deal about the characters who speak it, and the account of the conversation at the meal table is a comic highlight of the book; much of the comedy springs from the fact that so many different things are being talked about, all at the same time and in the same place. It is also very realistic.

Notice also in this chapter a feature of Wells's style, the way in which he can move suddenly from comic description of people and what they say, to serious paragraphs, such as when Mr Polly remembers or thinks about his dead father. The effect of this sudden change might be to confuse us, but in general the serious paragraphs are made more touching by the fact that we are surprised by them. The unfeeling, trivial nature of the other people at the funeral makes the serious paragraphs seem more serious by comparison, and the serious paragraphs, by showing us genuine feelings, emphasise just how silly the other guests can be.

NOTES AND GLOSSARY:

bric-à-brac: odds and ends, assorted bits

economist: not used here in its usual sense, but meaning someone mean with money

skylarked: played happily

Crystal Palace pantomime: the Crystal Palace was a giant building constructed largely of glass and iron between 1852–5; it was built out of materials used to construct the Exhibition Centre in London in 1851, and was a very popular entertainment centre, from 1854 to 1936. Pantomime is a form of theatre for children

up-line: Johnson sold tickets for those going 'up' to London on the railway

British Weekly: a non-denominational church magazine, started in 1866

Funerial baked meats: a reference to a line in Shakespeare's *Hamlet*, where Hamlet suggests that the hot food prepared for the funeral of Hamlet's father was served cold at his widow's wedding which followed on quickly

vulturial: a vulture is a bird that feeds on dead flesh, and Mr Polly is thinking of the relations who will come to the funeral simply for the food and the drink they will receive

mourning: black mourning clothes

Come the Heavy: act as if he had much better prospects of a job than he actually did

nest egg: money put to one side for use in emergencies

Fiancianier: for financier

floriferous: covered with flowers

Sundayfied: dressed in their best clothes for Sunday

spick and span: clean and neat

scrolly: ornate, richly decorated

dandled: to dandle is to play with a young baby, bounce him up and down on one's knee

Gals in service?: he is asking if the girls are employed as domestic servants

post mortem: (*Latin*) after death; the medical examination of a dead body, in order to find the cause of death

Hysterial catechunations: for hysterical cachinnations (waves of hysterical laughter)

bumping business: the coffin with Mr Polly's father in it would have been laid out in an upstairs room. The 'bumping business' is the noise made bringing it downstairs

mort: large number

chars:	does other people's housework for money
Dressed up to the nines:	dressed in their very best clothes
borryd:	borrowed
brawn:	meat
swaller:	swallow
Lemme:	let me
stummick:	stomach
mustid:	mustard
golp:	gulp, swallow noisily
audible ingurgitation:	very loud eating of food
snacks:	slang for rude remarks
get the Chuck:	be dismissed from his job

Chapter 5: Romance

Mr Polly is dismissed from his job because he stayed too long for the funeral, but this does not disturb him. He decides to have 'a little holiday', using some of the money left him by his father, but cannot trace Parsons, with whom he would have liked to spend his holiday. He goes to stay with the Johnsons, and buys a bicycle on which he rides round the countryside. He visits the Larkins with increasing frequency, and is made welcome at their house. On one of his bicycle rides, he meets and falls in love with a schoolgirl, but is only able to have brief conversations with her. He is deeply hurt when she brings some friends of hers to listen to her conversation with him, and feels that she has been mocking him.

COMMENTARY: This chapter emphasises the gap that exists between Mr Polly's dreams, and the reality of his, and other people's, lives. Mr Polly's dream world is represented by the books he buys, romantic, exciting, and adventurous. The real world is represented by Johnson, who thinks that Mr Polly should have invested his money in a book on how to keep accounts. Mr Polly wants fun, but all the world offers is business. He also wants companionship, and his desperate need for this leads him to overlook the faults of the Larkins, and see only the warmth and companionship they offer. This is also why he makes his mistake with the schoolgirl. She is a combination of all the things for which he yearns; she is romantic and exciting, and in addition offers him the friendship he so desperately wants. Mr Polly should learn from his mistake with the schoolgirl, but his being so badly hurt merely makes him tie himself even more strongly to the Larkins.

The episode with the schoolgirl is one of the more serious in the book, but Wells is careful not to let the scene get too serious. It hurts Mr Polly, certainly, but the reader is very much aware that the girl is just a schoolgirl, and that she cannot be entirely blamed if, at the end, she behaves like a schoolgirl. It is as much Mr Polly's fault as hers; he asks a young girl to respond to him as might a fully-grown woman.

NOTES AND GLOSSARY:

ante-separated: for anticipated

Mr Richard le Gallienne: Le Gallienne (1866–1947), a poet and novelist, popular in the 1890s

Theleme: an abbey in Rabelais' *Gargantua and Pantagruel* (1532). It is filled with high-born ladies and gentlemen, engaged in a continual round of festivities

Harold Johnsonese: Mr Polly told Mr Johnson about his thoughts in the sort of plain, matter-of-fact, and business-like language that was all Johnson could understand

Tales from Blackwood: a literary magazine, containing short stories. It was started in Edinburgh in 1817 and still flourishes

Purchas his Pilgrimes: a book by Samuel Purchas, published in 1625, based on the voyages of Richard Hakluyt, an Elizabethan voyager and explorer

The Life and Death of Jason: a long poem by William Morris (1834–96), published in 1866

book-keeping: accountancy

there is no may in early May: in May, which is meant to be a summer month, the climate and growth of plants are often nearer to that expected in winter

Exploratious menanderings: for exploratory meanderings

on the 'Op: for 'on the hop', slang phrase meaning unprepared, taken by surprise

wabble: for wobble

accidentulous: for accidental

prodic: for periodic

blump: possibly for 'plump', but more likely an attempt to suggest a rather soggy 'bump' sound

debreece: for debris

jawbacious: slang, meaning wordy, loud, wrangling

Infuriacious: for infuriating, extremely annoying

Swelpme: for so help me

friskiacious palfrey: for frisky horse

wreckery-ation ground: for recreation ground or park

Japanese lantern: lantern made of thin paper and wood; not the ideal bicycle lamp!

four-ale: beer that cost fourpence a quart

rum stuff: odd or unusual

oscoolatory exercises: for osculatory: kissing
strategical: related to the art of warfare
intrudacious: for intruding
retrospectatiousness: for retrospection, looking back on the past
chivalresque: for chivalrous
absquatulate: American slang, meaning to go away
gesticulatious: for gesticulatory, using expressive gestures, and meaning to carry on a relationship by sign-language such as waving arms
dillententytating: acting like a dilettante, someone who cannot make his mind up to anything
Gurdrum: heroine of an early German epic poem, and a symbol of loyalty, endurance, and love

---

Chapter 6: Miriam

Hurt and dismayed, Mr Polly goes back to the Larkins, and, without quite realising how it has come about, he finds himself engaged to marry Miriam. In desperation, he gets a small shop in Fishbourne, and has continual doubts and worries about the forthcoming marriage. However, the wedding goes ahead, under the watchful eyes of Mr Voules, a 'Larkins uncle', who organises it as efficiently as the Johnsons had organised the funeral of Mr Polly's father. After the wedding and reception for the guests, Mr and Mrs Polly depart on the train to their new home.

COMMENTARY: Wells hints strongly that Mr Polly marries Miriam only because he knows so few women: 'the number of women in his world was limited'. He thinks he has neglected the Larkins for 'a mirage' (the schoolgirl), but does not realise that the Larkins are another mirage, equally unlikely to provide what he really wants from life. His desire for excitement leads him on until he finds he has proposed to Miriam, although he never actually asks her specifically to marry him; it is just 'understood'. We see again that there is a streak of impetuosity in Mr Polly. We see also the likely fate of his shop when he tells Johnson 'There's no need to keep accounts . . .'; there is, although he does not realise it. Right from the start he has grave doubts about whether or not Miriam will make a good wife for him, but we see the same pattern in his marriage which has been visible in his whole life: he is caught up in events and swept forward by them, powerless to stop or alter what is happening. If Mr Polly's reaction to his impending marriage were not enough to tell us that it would be a disaster, the reaction of Mr Johnson and Uncle Pentstemon take it beyond doubt. They are both full of gloom at the prospect.

Wells's dislike of the Church of England comes through in his description of the marriage service. With the attitude of the vicar, Mrs Larkins's behaviour, and the devilish little boys with their rice, the whole ceremony hovers on the brink of farce. The reception after the service is almost identical to the one after the funeral (it even has many of the same people), and in Mr Voules we see again Wells's skill at creating brief but very telling characters out of simple physical description, and reproduction of their own style of speech. The connection with the earlier funeral service is not an accident; this marriage will almost prove the death of Mr Polly's dreams and happiness. The chapter ends on a note of anti-climax; Mr Polly's first passionate advances towards Miriam after the wedding are met with the reply, 'Be careful of my 'at.'

NOTES AND GLOSSARY:

keerless: for careless

delikit: for delicate

scraze: scratch

dogs'-eared: with the corners of pages turned down

Meditatious: for meditative

piece-work: the system whereby labourers are paid according to how much they produce, and not by the amount of time they spend working

Tabby: the most common kind of cat in Great Britain, usually grey or brown, with dark stripes

Fervous: for fervent, meaning ardent, earnest

'sturtiums: for nasturtiums (a type of flower)

Tom cat: male cat

reely: really

rum 'un: an odd or strange person

Delphicums: delphiniums (flowers)

Geezer: slang, meaning useless old man

nosey: slang, meaning careful

ex div.: after payment of dividend, the profit owing to a person who has invested money in shares or commerce

Vorterex: for vortex

debonairious: for debonair, meaning suave, courteous, well-dressed

chiffonier: a cupboard that could open up into a desk

double entry: a system of accounting in which each item of expenditure or income is entered twice in separate account books

contraption: business

Benedictine collapse: an obscure remark. Benedictine monks swore vows of celibacy, and Benedick was a character in Shakespeare's *Much Ado About Nothing* who professed to hate women, but ended up getting married at the end of the play. This remark by Mr Polly could refer to either, or it may be meaningless

amoor: (*French*) 'amour', love-affair

sotto voce: (*Italian*) in a low voice; neither of the Johnsons approve of the marriage, and so Mr Johnson is determined not to show too much enthusiasm

high-hung dogcart: a cart with fashionable high seats

Early Norman: a style of building with rounded window arches

Perpendicular: pointed arches in the Gothic style; despite knowing the correct terms, Mr Polly obviously does not know what they mean; the two styles are totally different

Telessated: presumably he means tessellated, in a mosaic pattern

D'bloved . . .: Wells is here being highly satirical about the speed and slackness with which the priest mouths the words of the Anglican marriage service. The actual words are these: Dearly beloved, we are gathered together here in the sight of God, and in the face of this congregation, to join together this Man and this Woman in Holy Matrimony; which is an honourable estate, instituted of God in the time of Man's innocency./ Wilt thou love her, comfort her, honour, and keep her in sickness and in health?/ Who giveth this Woman to be married to this Man?/ (*Repeat after me*) I take thee Miriam to my wedded wife, to have and to hold from this day forward, for better for worse, for richer for poorer./ With this ring I thee wed

Lego: let go

gothering: have you got the ring?

registry: for register

Ginn: an obsolete device for catching fish

éclat: (*French*) splendour, or with striking effect

auditory lodgement: making him hear

Got it in the back for a moment: the 'it' means a pain. Uncle Pentstemon suffers from rheumatism or arthritis, and believes that twinges in his muscles mean a change in the weather

passel: parcel

Vallyble:	valuable
uset':	used
loafer:	someone waiting around with nothing to do
hoss:	horse
Verbum sap:	(*Latin: verbum sapiente*) meaning one word is enough for a wise man
grub:	food
old Tommy:	port wine
Vociferatious:	for vociferous, meaning loud or noisy
nubblicks:	little bits
stummick:	stomach
worrit:	worry
grinny:	someone always grinning, silly
Wimmin:	women
a pig in a poke:	English saying, referring to someone who buys something without knowing very much about what it is he has actually purchased
grizzler:	a nagging, peevish person
liefer:	rather
lump-about:	someone who moves clumsily
en route:	(*French*) on the way
second class:	British Railways used to offer three classes on their trains: first, second, and third. First class was the most luxurious, and expensive. Today there are only two classes, first and second

---

Chapter 7: The Little Shop at Fishbourne

We have jumped fifteen years, and are back with Mr Polly as we first saw him at the start of the book: fat, unhealthy, and unhappy. From the start, Miriam disliked the shop and its living quarters, and became 'meagre and serious'. His only pleasure is reading (Miriam thinks this is simply him being lazy), and he has arguments and fights with all the neighbouring shopkeepers. He is 'bored to death with his business and his home and Miriam', and, sitting on his stile, he decides that the only way out is to commit suicide.

COMMENTARY: One of the basic ideas in *The History of Mr Polly* is that the members of Mr Polly's class are powerless to alter or influence their lives, and this is emphasised in this chapter by showing us Mr Polly enduring fifteen years of drudgery and boredom, without being able to change it. We are also reminded that fun and companionship, the two things Mr Polly most needs, are not available to him. Yet we do not blame the host of shopkeepers and other minor figures who flit through this chapter for their hostile reaction to Mr Polly, firstly because they are as helpless as he is, and secondly because Mr Polly was obviously capable of being an infuriating person. He may be the hero of the book, but Wells never hides his weaknesses and shortcomings from us. He may even be lazy, as Miriam says, and he is certainly a dreamer, and totally impractical. One of the questions you must ask yourself, and one which Wells himself seems a little unclear about, is whether Mr Polly's predicament is his fault, or the fault of society. The answer may well be that both are partially to blame.

This chapter shows again Wells's skill in character-sketch and in dialogue. Mr Polly's deteriorating relationships with his wife and neighbours are beautifully described, in a manner that is at one and the same time tragic and comic; comic, because in incidents like the fight between Mr Polly and Rusper both men behave in a very silly and petty way, but also tragic, because such incidents are born out of desperation and frustration.

Twice in this chapter Wells digresses, and moves away from straightforward telling of the story. He talks at some length about the books Mr Polly has read, and gives at even greater length a lecture on the sociological views of his contemporary, Sidney Webb. Wells has been criticised for thus breaking away from his story, and it would be rare to find this sort of thing in a modern novel. However, it was still an accepted technique in Wells's day, and the conventions of novel writing allowed the author to appear much more frequently in his work than would be the case nowadays. Also, both digressions are relevant to the book. You must decide yourself whether these passages help you to understand and enjoy the book, or whether they act as distractions, making the book less real and true-to-life.

NOTES AND GLOSSARY:

hat-guards: pieces of material that clipped a hat to a jacket, so that it could not be carried away in a strong wind

zealacious: for zealous, meaning with energy and enthusiasm

Obi: African spell used to cause ill-health and death

job lot: mixed or unsorted collection, sold at auctions

La Perouse: a French explorer who lived from 1741 to 1788

The Island Nights' Entertainment: three stories by Robert Louis Stevenson (1850–94), published in 1893

Fenimore Cooper: American novelist (1789–1851), whose best novels were about Red Indians

Tom Cringle's Log: a sea story for boys, by Michael Scott (1789–1851)

Sterne: Laurence Sterne (1713–68), eccentric clergyman and one of England's greatest comic novelists, author of *Tristram Shandy* (1759–67) and *A Sentimental Journey* (1768)

Lever: Charles Lever (1806–72), an Irish novelist, very popular in the nineteenth century

Scott: Sir Walter Scott (1771–1832), famous Scottish historical novelist. Wells disliked Scott's work

Joyce: James Joyce (1882–1941), Irish novelist and poet, author of *Dubliners* (1914), *A Portrait of the Artist as a Young Man* (1916), *Ulysses* (1922), and *Finnegans Wake* (1939)

Only those areas are glossed where Wells gives a title but no author, or an author without any book title, to make identification easier. It is the fact that Mr Polly read at all that is significant, not so much what he actually read. The only links between these many and various titles are that a number of them are tales by explorers and adventurers, deal with far-away places, or are adventure stories designed for young boys. Many of the authors are 'modern', at least as far as Wells was concerned.

cinque cento: (*Italian*) of the sixteenth century

ruffling: wild, bustling

a certain high-browed gentleman: Sidney Webb (1859–1947), a sociologist and contemporary of Wells's. Though Wells did not like Webb, he agreed with his theories

vertebracious: referring to the fact that Man is a vertebrate animal

Arreary Pensy: *arrière-pensée* (*French*), meaning afterthought

stror: straw

lemme: let me

pavemint: pavement

no truck: any business

equestrian proclivities: an interest in horse-racing and betting

softish sort of flat: a weak and boring person

flapping your mouth: talking to other people, being a gossip

pugginess: thickness, weight

Berlin wool: knitting wool

cinematograph peep-show: a display of early and primitive photographs

the German peril: the threat to Great Britain posed by Germany, now a large industrial nation, and rival to Britain in her economy and her armed forces. War was to break out between the two in 1914

William: Kaiser Wilhelm II (1859–1941), ruler of Germany, who was deposed in 1918

Xerxiacious: Mr Polly is referring to Xerxes (519–465BC), an early and immensely powerful King of Persia, who invaded Greece in 481. His great army was opposed by the famous three hundred at Thermopylae, his fleet destroyed at Salamis and he retired to Asia

Jer doing?:	What are you doing?
Leggo:	let go
midriff:	stomach
concavity:	between stomach and chest
Jiu-jitsu:	Ju-jitsu, a system of unarmed combat, Japanese in origin
scrags:	a slang phrase, meaning attacks

Chapter 8: Making an End to Things

Mr Polly plans his suicide with great care, deciding to burn down the shop and then cut his own throat. It has to appear to be an accident, because the insurance company will not pay out to Miriam if it appears that the whole thing was deliberate. All goes well until Mr Polly's trousers catch fire in the blaze he has started. In panic, he forgets to cut his throat, and rescues an old lady from Mr Rumbold's burning shop. He is a hero, doubly so because the shopkeepers whose shops have been burnt down are delighted to have their loss-making businesses replaced by hard cash from the insurance companies. Mr Polly's fictitious story about how the fire started is believed by everybody.

COMMENTARY: This chapter marks a turning-point in the story of Mr Polly. For the first time in his life, he takes matters into his own hands, and actually does something that alters his prospects for the better. Of course, it is not what he planned to do, but that is simply Wells being realistic. We know too much about Mr Polly to expect his plans to work out to the last detail.

The description of the great Fishbourne fire is a comic masterpiece. Wells evokes the chaos and confusion of the scene with masterful skill, combining vivid description of the scene with comic description of the individuals involved in the fire. We are able to enjoy the description of the fire (which could, after all, be a tragic event) because Wells keeps up the comic tone throughout, thus reassuring us that there will be no deaths or real disasters as a result of the fire. When he goes to bed that night, Mr Polly is a new man.

NOTES AND GLOSSARY:

mope:	be in a miserable state
holler:	cry out
arsonical:	like arson, the wilful or criminal burning of buildings or property
pinged:	made a brief ringing noise
recrudescent:	burning up again
Ramadan:	the name given to the month during which all Muslims fast from break of dawn to sunset

weekly interlude . . . imposes:	the time on Sunday when the law required public houses and inns to be shut
hobbledehoys:	workmen
Tariff Reform:	the subject of much political discussion at the time of writing, it was essentially a method of protecting British trade against foreign competition, by imposing tariffs on all imports
Gud!:	God
manual:	a hand-operated fire engine
longshoremen:	dock-workers
parleyed:	talked (from French *parler*)
snakes/worms:	the hoses belonging to Mr Rusper
écru:	pale, whitish
Shinning:	climbing
Urup!:	hurry up!
Gollys!:	a mild expletive, or swear word
Sich:	such
Lawks-a-mussy!:	another mild expletive, literally 'Lord have mercy!'
git:	get
carm:	come
wuss:	worse
fust:	first
anon:	occasionally, every now and then
'white man':	a good fellow
dress trousers:	trousers worn as part of formal evening wear
shooting of coals:	the noise coal makes as it is loaded into a cellar
Gladstone-shaped:	a high, stiff collar
Phoenix:	a bird in Egyptian mythology that rejuvenated itself by burning on its own funeral pyre

---

Chapter 9: The Potwell Inn

Having seen that he can alter his future, Mr Polly decides to 'clear out'. He decides to go rambling through the countryside, leaving Miriam with all the insurance money, except twenty-one pounds, which he will keep for himself. For almost the first time in his life, he is healthy, happy, and stimulated.

Eventually Mr Polly arrives at the Potwell Inn, and is offered a job there as general odd-job man by its fat landlady. He meets Polly, the landlady's granddaughter, and hears about the terrible Uncle Jim, a violent criminal who is extorting money from the landlady, and threatening violence to her. After a considerable internal struggle, Mr Polly decides to stay and fight it out with Jim. With the aid of a broom, a lot of running away, and considerable luck, Mr Polly drives Jim into the river at their first violent encounter. The second time they meet, it is a combination of Mr Polly and the guests at the inn who drive Jim off. The third time, the gun Jim is using blows up, and he leaves again, this time taking Mr Polly's clothes with him.

COMMENTARY: One of the things that Mr Polly has to learn is stated very early on in this chapter: 'If the world does not please you, *you can change it*.' True, Wells admits that this change need not be for the better, but the mere possibility of change is enough to cheer up Mr Polly.

A feature of Wells's style that appears in this chapter, and throughout the book, is his use of real place-names, such as Tunbridge Wells and Maidstone. Though the story is fictional, many of the places mentioned in it are not, and this adds to the effect of reality that Wells creates. However, we have already seen that his digressions and tendency to lecture the reader could make the book more unreal, and some critics think that the happy ending of the book has the same effect. It is certainly true that when Mr Polly becomes a tramp and wanders the roads of England, it is only the happier side of such an existence that we see, and the cold, illness, and occasional violence that went with such a way of life are not mentioned.

Uncle Jim could almost be said to exist because, without a figure like him, the final chapters would be too idyllic, and Mr Polly's conversion to a new life far too easy to be credible. The world portrayed in the earlier chapters of *The History of Mr Polly* is cruel and harsh, and that cruelty and harshness is represented by Jim. Nevertheless, critics have also accused Wells of painting too perfect a picture of the countryside, ignoring its drawbacks as much as he exaggerates the problems of living in a town.

The fat landlady is the exact opposite of Miriam: fat, basically happy and cheerful, and a tender companion, where Miriam was thin, sour, and a nagging wife.

In the battles between Jim and Mr Polly, we again see Wells's skill in writing set-piece comic scenes, where quite large numbers of people are involved in a dramatic incident. If there is comedy in the chapter, there is also a serious element, Wells's criticism of the penal system, which in Uncle Jim's case sent him to a so-called Reformatory that was nothing more than a school for criminals.

NOTES AND GLOSSARY:

Toad Rock: a rock shaped like a toad; a rock like this did exist, at a village called Rusthall, in Wiltshire, England

plump equatorially: fat round the middle

Aurora Borealis: also known as the 'Northern Lights', this is a display of colour sometimes seen in the sky a few hours after sunset

taps:	rooms for drinking in public houses, so called because of the 'taps' from which the beer was drawn
casual ward:	a rough hostel for tramps and other vagrants, where the person could stay for one night only. These had a very bad reputation at the time, which is perhaps why Mr Polly only stayed for one night in one
Itchabod:	for Ichabod, meaning 'the glory is departed'. See the Bible, I Samuel 4:21
Provinder:	for provender, food, sustenance
beer engine:	a machine for drawing up the beer from its barrel
Shrub:	a drink containing a mixture of rum and fruit juice
Toby jug:	a ceramic jug, made in the shape of an old man wearing a large hat
Assumption-ing Madonna:	a painting of the Virgin Mary being received into Heaven on her death, and after the death of Christ; another example of Wells being rude, and possibly offensive, about religion
Oooooover!:	Over; someone is calling for the ferryman to carry him over the river
Sumpthing:	for something
dessay:	dare say
Wax to receive and marble to retain:	a saying, meaning willing to learn, and able to retain what has been learnt
lear:	empty, hollow
Ceteris paribus?:	(*Latin*) 'all things being equal', but used by Mr Polly to mean 'and other things'
Reformatory:	a prison for young criminals
Stockholm tarring:	painting with tar
garing:	making ready for the road
scooted:	got rid of
scorcher:	slang, meaning someone to be admired
Drorback:	drawback
Words:	the implication is that it is foul language Uncle Jim is teaching her
licence:	the landlady's licence to run the inn depends on her providing an efficient ferry service
Herculaceous:	like Hercules, a hero in Greek mythology who possessed immense strength. This word is Mr Polly's own invention
bicepitally:	referring to the biceps, muscles in the upper arm. Another Polly invention
shillin':	shilling, an old unit of currency, worth five pence

Sumpthing: something, used as a term of abuse
lime-juice people: the suppliers of lime-juice to the inn
'Arf a mo': slang, meaning half a minute: wait for a short while
noo bloke: new man
sanguinary/decorated: the words in brackets replace the swear words that Jim was using
Marathon: a long athletic race, commemorating the legendary runner who, in 490BC, brought the news of the Athenians' victory over the Persians led by Darius by running the 42 km from the battlefield at Marathon to Athens. The race is one of the most challenging events of the Olympic Games
cinder track: athletics track, made of fine cinders
jest: just
wiv: with
blurry: bloody, a swear word
beat: area, territory
shift: move out
nuffin: nothing
orf: off
uvver: other
cadger: beggar, scrounger
stummick: stomach
spirituous reek: smell of alcohol
Bolls!: bottles
soul-blenching: enough to make the soul go white with fear
chess: chest
Lea go!: let go
the heel of Achilles: the weak point. Achilles, a Greek hero, was invulnerable to attack or wounds except in his heel; he was eventually killed by such a wound
worter: water
marrer: bone marrow; deep inside his bones
alcolaceous: alcoholic; a Polly invention
conversazione: (*Italian*) conversation
noosance: nuisance
Territorials: part-time soldiers
à la carte: (*French*) a menu from which separate items can be chosen
'prentices: apprentices
benifluous: for beneficent
chunk: a large lump
decolletage: in an open-necked shirt
ox-hide shield: a primitive shield, covered in ox-hide

parasol:	sun-shade, umbrella
Suffragettes:	women who were fighting to gain equal rights with men, in areas such as voting and property ownership. Some of their meetings were violent
ferrule:	stick
lagged:	sent to prison
munce:	months
rook rifle:	small-bore rifle

Chapter 10: Miriam Revisited

After five happy years at the Potwell Inn, Mr Polly's conscience begins to trouble him over Miriam, and he goes back to see her. She is now running a tea-shop in Fishbourne with her sister Annie, and is horrified when she meets him. Mr Polly decides to leave her in peace, as she obviously neither wants nor needs him. He goes back to the Potwell Inn, knowing that the final cloud on his horizon has been removed. Jim has drowned, wearing Mr Polly's clothes, and has been so disfigured in the water that he has been identified as Mr Polly; hence Miriam's tea-shop, bought with the help of the money from Mr Polly's life insurance.

Returning to the inn, he seems set for a happy and contented life.

COMMENTARY: The purpose of this brief concluding chapter is to tie up loose ends, and conclude the novel on a happy note. It is necessary for us to know that Miriam is not suffering by Mr Polly's absence, because if she were, then Mr Polly would appear to us as a mean figure, and the cause of that suffering. Although Wells has never been afraid in the novel to point out Mr Polly's weaknesses, he is a person with whom we are meant to feel some sympathy. Similarly, we must know that Uncle Jim will never return if we are to believe in Mr Polly's continuing happiness at the Potwell Inn.

Another point of interest in the chapter is Wells's attitude to arson, or at least, Mr Polly's arson. He dismisses it as unimportant, and even praiseworthy. It may seem strange to find an eminent novelist appearing to favour illegal acts, but the philosophy behind this attitude is consistent with other remarks Wells has made during the course of the book. This philosophy is basically the idea that what matters is how we treat people, not how we treat things. Seen in this light, the destruction of a number of ugly shops, to the benefit of their owners, is not a crime. What Wells seems to ignore is the fact that any arsonist runs the risk of killing someone, whether he means to or not. Mr Polly's crime is not serious, in human terms; Wells would be at fault if he made it appear that all arson is equally harmless.

NOTES AND GLOSSARY:

Swiss Teutonic style:	the German/Swiss style, with low, overhanging roof and a balcony
a lottery:	a game of chance
absquatulate:	to decamp or go away
skeptacious:	for sceptical
nigger:	negro
black nettle pagodas:	nettle plants shaped like pagodas, sacred ornately carved temples found in Eastern countries
diaphalous:	for diaphanous, transparent

Part 3

Commentary

Plot and structure

The plot of a novel is its story, and the plot of *The History of Mr Polly* is often described as loose and sprawling, more a string of incidents than the scrupulously planned structure usually associated with the word plot.

These criticisms are often the result of the critic comparing the book with the Victorian type of novel, which often had a very complex plot. In such a novel, the story might be very long, and contain many different incidents and episodes. The novel was often built round a series of climaxes, carefully prepared, and finishing with one great climax where events were brought to a close and the whole truth about the particular situation that the novel dealt with revealed. Large numbers of characters were usually introduced, and their individual fortunes followed with care and attention throughout the book.

The History of Mr Polly is certainly not like this. There are climaxes in the book, such as the dismissal of Parsons and the death of Mr Polly's father, but the two major climaxes are bunched together at the end of the novel (the fire, and the battle with Uncle Jim), and there is a section in the middle of the book, comprising Chapters 5, 6 and 7, in which there are no major climaxes. Indeed, the events talked about in these chapters (Mr Polly's 'holiday', his marriage, and the shop at Fishbourne) are more of an anti-climax, since none of them live up to Mr Polly's expectations. Large numbers of characters are introduced in the book, but they are then often forgotten about, and never appear again; Parsons, Platt, and Mr Voules are examples of this. Right at the end of his novel, Wells is still introducing new characters, like the fat landlady and Uncle Jim. Once they have served their purpose in the novel, characters are dropped, and, with a very few exceptions, we never hear what has happened to them since. Nor are we told very much about what their lives had been like before the events narrated in the book.

In addition to all this, Wells starts his novel in the middle of the story, and thereby can be accused of lessening tension, as we already know part of what is to be told after a few pages. He casually jumps fifteen years in a few lines, and at the end transfers his story to a totally new setting, that of the Potwell Inn. All these things might suggest that the plot of the book is a rambling, confused, and rather disorganised affair. However, this is not entirely the case.

The plot of *The History of Mr Polly* should not be compared with that of Victorian novels, but goes back to an earlier style of novel, the picaresque. The first picaresque novel was Cervantes' *Don Quixote* (1603) and the name for this kind of novel comes from the Spanish word given to its hero, the *pícaro*, or rogue. In English, the first great picaresque novel was Fielding's *Tom Jones* (1749). In the picaresque novel, the central figure or hero (the *pícaro*) goes out journeying into the world, and the novel tells the story of the things that happen to him on his journey. Thus the plot is simply a string of incidents, often linked only by the fact that the central figure appears in each incident. *The History of Mr Polly* is not a picaresque novel in the strict sense of the word, because Mr Polly's journeying is quite limited, and he has no servant or helper to accompany him, but the plot of the book follows the picaresque pattern in that its only unifying factor is the central character himself. We do not feel lost or confused in the book, because everything that happens tells us more about Mr Polly and increases our understanding of him. Thus the Victorian novel needed its complex plot to balance and sustain an examination of several characters; Wells has only one character, and everything in the novel must serve the single purpose of telling us more about him. The danger is that if Wells introduces too many characters and incidents the reader might lose sight of Mr Polly, but this does not happen.

Starting his story in the middle has a number of advantages for Wells. It is a dramatic opening, and one that gains our attention, for it is obvious that Mr Polly is in the middle of a major crisis, and we automatically want to see how this is going to be resolved. Also, the first part of Mr Polly's life is a story of failure and depression; the opening of the book tells us that a moment of truth will occur, whereas if we did not know this we might assume that all Mr Polly's life would follow this pattern of failure, and perhaps lose interest as a result. In other words, the opening of the novel does not lessen the tension, but increases it, by forewarning us that a major crisis will come in Mr Polly's life, and that major decisions will have to be taken. Starting in the middle of the story was a device favoured by the great classical writers in their epic poetry.

The plot of *The History of Mr Polly* is not as tightly organised as that of many Victorian novels, but Wells can afford to be more relaxed over the way he links his incidents together, because the incidents are of secondary importance to the central character. Although there are weaknesses in the plot, like the lectures we occasionally receive from the author, and the rather blank patch in the middle of the book, they do not damage in any significant way the fresh and invigorating picture that we receive of the central character, Mr Polly.

Themes

The themes of a novel are the subjects in it which an author looks at or examines in some depth, often with a view to making some sort of serious comment on them. Thus a theme can be defined as the central idea, or ideas, which run through a work. In *The History of Mr Polly* the themes include the plight of the lower middle class, the ability of an individual to influence his own destiny, the problems of middle age, and the appalling state of English education. Some modern criticism tends to concentrate on themes, and view them as the most important element in literature. This is unwise; themes are important, but so are characterisation, style, comic technique, and all the other factors that go to make a great novel.

The plight of the lower middle class

It is often very difficult for someone who has not lived in England to understand the English class system, and difficult sometimes even for those who have. The class which Wells is most concerned with in *The History of Mr Polly* is the lower middle class, one grade above the working class in the social scale. The working class of Wells's day can be defined as wage-earners involved largely in manual labour, and earning relatively little. Factory and farm workers were the largest group in this class, although domestic servants, of which there were a vast number, can also be included. The lower middle class was a relatively new group in Wells's time, and had been on the increase for a number of years as a result of the Industrial Revolution. Many were from working-class backgrounds, and were trying to fight their way up the social ladder. Many were wage-earners, like the working class, but were distinguished from them by the fact that their jobs did not normally involve manual labour. Instead, they worked in offices as clerks, or held minor clerical positions in the railways, like Harold Johnson; they were shop assistants, or the owners of small shops, like Mr Polly.

Wells concentrates attention on these people by writing about the views of Sidney Webb, that 'certain high-browed gentleman living at Highbury', and Wells's concern about them is visible throughout the book. The only difference between the views held by Wells and those held by Webb is that Wells thought Webb too clinical and inhumane, and not sufficiently aware of the human element in the problems he presented. The main elements in their combined view are these: the lower middle class is a new phenomenon, brought about as the result of industrialisation making more wealth available. Because it is a new class, it has few roots in the community, and no sense of history to make its members feel a part of society. Their aim is to climb out of the drudgery and misery of working-class existence, but as they have relatively little money, there are strict limitations on the way in which they can do this, and they are not helped by being badly educated and thoroughly ill-prepared for leading any sort of productive existence. The small shops or businesses which are all they can afford are a waste of resources. The services they provide are not really necessary to the community, and there are so many of them that their efforts are duplicated and their value lessened even further. They are wasteful of resources, because they are badly run, and because the people who own and run them could benefit society much more by being diverted to other, more productive and useful jobs. The lower middle class is therefore like a parasite on the body of society, drawing things out of it but giving nothing valuable in return.

Wells examines all this in his novel, and it must have been a matter of great concern to him, as well as one of personal experience, for his own parents had made this climb from domestic servant to shopkeeper. He shows us the miserable education that fails to equip the lower middle class for anything, the aimless, rootless existence of its members and the essentially unproductive life that they lead. But where Webb was content to condemn, Wells shows us the people behind the social problem, the Pollys and Ruspers who are the real lower middle class. They yearn for better things, but some are caught 'like rabbits in a net', unable to stop a slow slide into poverty and depression. In all tragedies there is a feeling of inevitability, of men caught up in events that they cannot foresee or control, and which lead eventually to their ruin. Although *The History of Mr Polly* is not a tragedy, there is enough of this feeling in it to give it tragic overtones. However, it is the comic side of the lower middle class that is uppermost in the book, and though Wells has considerable sympathy for the members of this class, as befits someone who was once a member of it himself, he can also see the funny side of their attempts to come to terms with their existence. Hence the book is a tragicomedy, a blend of the two modes, with the comedy dominant.

Wells can see and sympathise with the problems of the lower middle class; what he cannot do is offer a wide-ranging solution to these problems. His solution depends totally on individual effort allied with luck, and applies only to Mr Polly; it could not be applied to the class as a whole. In this area at least there may be some justification for those critics who say that Wells's outlook is limited: while he can see that problems exist, he cannot work out effective solutions to them.

The power of the individual

Another major theme of the novel is summed up in the sentence, 'If the world does not please you, *you can change it.*' Thus while Wells is not able to offer a mass solution to the problems of the lower middle class, he does at least offer some hope to individual members of it. Mr Polly, of course, is the example by which Wells shows us what can be done, but Wells is quite realistic about what this involves. He says that a determination to alter one's position in the world can lead to disaster as well as happiness, and he shows us, through Mr Polly, that luck plays no small part in a happy ending to this decision. It is not easy for Mr Polly to break out from the world in which he has lived for so long, and Wells suggests that one of the worst features of the sort of life that Mr Polly had been leading is the way in which its misery and boredom sap at the very roots of a man's spirit, and take away from him the drive and enthusiasm that could allow him to alter his future.

This raises the whole question of the relationship between a man and the society in which he lives, and this in turn leads on to one of the most popular examination questions on *The History of Mr Polly*: does the responsibility for the misery of Mr Polly's early life lie with society or with Mr Polly? In other words, who is to blame, Mr Polly or the society in which he lives, for the state in which we see him at the start of the novel?

In one sense, the question is answered by what has been said above; if the individual has it within his power to break out into a new life, then it is his fault if he does not do so, and not society's. However, this is only half an answer. An individual may be able to break out, but society, as we see it in *The History of Mr Polly*, does its best to stop him doing so. It educates him badly in a manner that destroys initiative and imagination, and does not prepare him for doing anything. It ties him to a bleak system of apprenticeship that further destroys his individuality. It punishes him for wrongdoing, but offers him no incentive to do well. The religion it offers him is a superficial nonsense, at least according to Wells, and at all times the individual is left alone, without help or understanding offered him by society.

However, Wells is too honest to say that it is all society's fault. Mr Polly has many faults as well, not all of them caused by society, and it is a combination of the two that leads to the frustration and despair of his early years. What does emerge from the novel is Wells's firm belief in the individual. He seems to be saying that whatever society, communities, or countries impose on people, a person still has the power to alter his own destiny, if he wants to sufficiently strongly. This is an optimistic view of human nature, although in his last years, Wells seemed to change to a more pessimistic outlook.

The problems of middle age

One of the reasons for the success of *The History of Mr Polly* is that Mr Polly is a representative figure; he is not just a figure in a novel, but someone whose problems represent those faced by many people. For this reason large numbers of readers have felt able to sympathise with him, as well as seeing in him some of their own weaknesses and frailties. Thus Mr Polly represents all those people who find themselves living lives for which they can feel no enthusiasm, and from which they gain no satisfaction; he also represents all those who have felt the need to 'clear out', and those who have done so. The reader can identify with him all the more easily because he is an ordinary man, not a perfect hero or an absolutely evil man; he is all the more realistic, and representative, for being fairly normal.

There is another area in which he is a representative figure. Middle age is often a difficult time. It is a time when people look back on their lives, and ask what they have achieved; it is also a time when the chance of doing anything new seems to be rapidly receding, and life can seem to be almost over. Mr Polly is in this position when we see him on his stile at the start of the book, and he faces both these problems in a very extreme manner. It must appear as if he has achieved nothing, and the chances of him altering this state of affairs appear to be non-existent. Wells provides hope for all those who have felt this way, or feel that they may do so in the future, by showing that a person's life is not finished at forty, and that he can still achieve worthwhile things after that age has been reached. This particular theme could perhaps be summed up in the old saying that while there is life, there is hope.

The countryside

A recurring theme in *The History of Mr Polly* is the beauty of the English countryside. in Chapter 1, Wells writes, 'There is no country-side like the English country-side for those who have learned to love it', and in Chapter 9 there are some beautiful descriptive passages, as Mr Polly rambles on his way to the Potwell Inn. However, Wells has been criticised for making his vision of the countryside too escapist and unreal.

There is some truth in this; there is a rather facile link in the novel between personal happiness and the countryside, but there are also at least two things which could by no stretch of the imagination be seen as happy, namely Christabel (the schoolgirl) and Uncle Jim. More to the point, there is a tendency nowadays to see all pictures of perfect rural landscapes as escapist and unreal. British society has come to be dominated by the industrial landscape; the majority of the population live in towns, and many of Britain's present problems are the result of industrialisation. It is therefore quite natural to demand that a writer face up to these modern problems, and not retreat into the countryside. On the other hand, just because a writer refuses to write wholly about the towns and cities does not mean to say that he is being unreal, or hiding from reality. Wells gives us a lot of detail about town life, and provides us with some beautiful paragraphs about the English landscape:

> He crossed some misty meadows by moonlight and the mist lay low on the grass, so low that it scarcely reached above his waist, and houses and clumps of trees stood out like islands in a milky sea, so sharply defined was the upper surface of the mist-bank. He came nearer and nearer to a strange thing that floated like a boat upon this magic lake, and behold, something moved at the stern, and a rope was whisked at the prow, and it had changed into a pensive cow, drowsy-eyed, regarding him ...

There is no great harm in it if Wells chooses to see the countryside as something that is 'as safe and enclosed and fearless as a child that has still to be born'.

Minor themes and the importance of people

There are a number of minor themes in the novel, amongst which must be numbered Wells's attacks on education, the Church, the apprenticeship system, and, in the case of Mr Polly's arson and insurance fraud, the law. These are minor themes because they do not occupy a large part of the book, but they have one thing in common: they are all attacked and criticised because in one way or another they work not for people, but against them, and damage individuals by removing from them their dignity, or their true abilities. From this we can see Wells's tremendous concern for the individual; indeed, one of the strongest statements made in *The History of Mr Polly* is that individual human beings are what matter in the world, and that anything that harms them is evil.

Disentanglement and the comedy of limitation

If you read other critical works on *The History of Mr Polly*, you may find references to the theme of disentanglement. All this means is that the book is about a man who tries to fight clear of the limitations imposed on him by a hostile society and his own deficiencies. Thus Mr Polly has to 'disentangle' himself from the mess he has got himself into. The term 'comedy of limitations' means much the same thing, except that in this phrase the word 'comedy' suggests that the story has a happy ending.

Of all the themes mentioned in the above section, which do you think is the most significant? Can you think of any possible themes that have been missed out from this discussion?

The characters

General points

There are several general points which can be made about Wells's technique of characterisation in *The History of Mr Polly*. One of these is that although there are a large number of characters in the book, they vary little in terms of status or ability. There are no great men in the book, no lords, rich men, or leaders of society, or even very many professional people like lawyers and doctors. Wells's characters are drawn almost exclusively from the lower middle class, and the majority of the people in his book are ordinary men and women, with no very remarkable features. This can be seen as a weakness, leading to a lack of variety and contrast in the novel, but it is also a strength. Wells has been seen as a champion of 'the common man', and there is no doubt that he can write about ordinary people extremely vividly. His characters may be ordinary, but one of the things that he succeeds in doing very well is showing us that an apparently ordinary and uninteresting man can have within him a range and variety of feelings that would not shame a military hero. There may be no great men in the street where Mr Polly's shop is situated, but there is a wide range of human character. There is thus variety in the characterisation, even if the characters tend to be drawn from the same social class. Remember that the narrator is another character in the book, and one who can often provide a viewpoint that is different from that shared by the characters in the book.

Wells's technique for portraying his characters is simple. He tends to introduce characters by means of a brief physical description, and thereafter relies heavily on their speech and their actions to tell us what they are like. Wells thus describes characters by their external appearance and actions (which is, of course, how we form our judgements of people in real life, and hence quite a realistic technique). He tells us quite often what Mr Polly is thinking, but with the other characters he is usually quite content to let us form our own conclusions on the basis of what we see them say and do. Occasionally, he will push us in the right direction by coming out into the open and telling us what to think of a character, as when he says of Miriam that she 'combined earnestness of spirit with great practical incapacity', but this is rare, and Wells does not tell us what is going on inside a character's head nearly as often as would a modern novelist.

Wells has been compared with Dickens, in that both authors tend to create a large number of characters, and link their characterisation of them to one single feature, often something odd or amusing. This technique of emphasising one feature in a character is often called caricature; the difference between Wells and Dickens is that the latter often exaggerates more, whereas the characteristic of a Wells character is often fairly ordinary, albeit highly descriptive: examples of this are Uncle Pentstemon's hollow tooth and his arthritis, Miriam's thinness, the landlady's fat, and the old lady's repeated assertion that she 'can't jump!'. Certainly Wells is attracted by an oddity in a character, such as Rusper's 'klik'. Wells has been accused of creating superficial characters who lack depth, but we can often work out quite a lot more about a character from what Wells tells us, without having to be told directly by him, and what we lack in depth we often make up for in sheer numbers.

Another two accusations commonly made against Wells are that he cannot write convincing or fair sketches of women, and that however complete his characters may be in themselves, he cannot show us them reacting against each other; in other words, each individual character is very isolated, and tends not to relate to other characters in the book. The first point is perhaps more a matter of taste; it is true that very few of the women in *The History of Mr Polly* come out of it with any great credit, but there are no rules to say that Wells must give an equal account of good and bad women in his novel, and the pictures of Miriam, the Larkins, and the others are certainly convincing, if often unpleasant. As regards the characters being isolated, it is partly a theme of the book that people often do not communicate effectively with each other; look at the scenes after the wedding and funeral, where each character is determined to express his or her point of view, and not really interested in what the others have to say. One of Mr Polly's great problems is that he cannot make other people understand his dreams and aspirations. Thus this feature, far from being a weakness, may be Wells trying to make a valid point.

Very few of the characters in *The History of Mr Polly* lack weaknesses. One of the great features of English comic writing has been the ability to laugh at weakness in a person, and yet sympathise with and understand it. By displaying a very accurate eye for the faults of his characters, yet displaying a tremendous love and tolerance of them (especially in Mr Polly), Wells puts himself amongst the ranks of the greatest English comic writers.

Mr Polly

Mr Polly is a plump, pleasant-faced man with nothing remarkable about his appearance, except perhaps the hats and silk ties that he sometimes wears from the stock in his shop. He is in quite good health, though run down by his manner of living, and he suffers chronically from indigestion; this is the result of being badly fed both by his mother and his wife, and is not helped by his fondness for pickles and highly flavoured foods. His indigestion is a symbol of his life; the almost permanent battle that is taking place inside his stomach reflects the conflict in his own mind and the conflict he faces with the outside world. It also colours his view of the world, and makes him even more depressed and miserable than he would otherwise have been.

He has imagination and curiosity, but his schooling tried to stamp out both these features. It failed to do so completely, but left him a confused and unsatisfied man, desperately wanting excitement, adventure, and romance in his life, but uncertain about where to find them, or even if they exist outside the pages of books. He is an avid reader, but indiscriminate in what he reads, and unable to put the knowledge he acquires to any good use. He is frightened of being made to look foolish, but likes to be the centre of attention, and both these features can be seen at work in his liking for big words, and inability to understand or pronounce them correctly.

He desperately wants companionship and love, and these are denied him for most of the book. The pressure for these things builds up so terribly inside him that in the end, he sees them where they do not actually exist, in the schoolgirl and in Miriam. He is not a very good judge of character, and makes enemies easily because he cannot express himself, and appears strange, and sometimes rude, to other people. He is easily flustered and readily excited in company, and is not at all a practical man, until genuine interest makes him so at the Potwell Inn. At times, he could be a brilliant salesman, but his lack of interest in the job of draper stops him from achieving his potential. He is a kind and well-meaning man, as we see in his rescue of the old lady and his troubled conscience over Miriam, but he is also weak-willed, with a strong tendency to try and run away from situations that he does not like; when he cannot run away, as on his wedding day, he lets events take their course. The turning-point is his confrontation with Uncle Jim, because here he overcomes his weak will and his tendency to run away from unpleasant situations, and lets himself be dominated by his better instincts.

He is a criminal, but we do not feel that we can condemn him for what he does. He is a man who above all needs an interest in life, warm friendship, and a home; it is not until he finds all three at the Potwell Inn that he can be happy. He is not a 'hero' in the usual sense of the word, but a weak and insignificant little man, but nevertheless one for whom we can feel strong sympathy, and whose weaknesses reflect those we know exist in ourselves.

Mr Polly is a shy dreamer, someone who has no desire for riches; but there are also two Mr Pollys in the book: the one before the Potwell Inn, and the one after. Before he has 'no Zest! no Vim!' and is 'feeble and weak'; after, he is, in his own words, like 'a Visitant from Another World'. The new Mr Polly has been there all along, but it needs a change of environment and attitude to bring him out into the open. The main crisis in the book is his decision to commit suicide; it is from this decision that the new Mr Polly springs, and we feel that he has earned his peace and contentment at the end of the novel, 'just mellowish and warmish like ....'

Parsons

Parsons, Mr Polly's fellow apprentice at Port Burdock and one of the 'three P's', is a plump, loud extrovert, bubbling over with ideas about literature, window dressing, and life. He is one of the few people in the novel who can in any way share Mr Polly's romantic notions about life and his love of books, and when he is dismissed for assaulting his employer, something very vital goes out of Mr Polly's life. It could almost be said that Mr Polly spends much of the rest of his life looking for someone like Parsons, and failing to find him.

The Johnson family

Harold Johnson is everything that Mr Polly is not: serious, practical, down-to-earth, and also totally boring. It is possible to blame Parsons for encouraging Mr Polly's romantic notions, but Johnson is more to blame for pushing Mr Polly into buying a shop, a decision that shows a total failure to understand Mr Polly. On the other hand, Johnson is infuriatingly well-meaning, and his life is dominated by a desire to do the right thing, and not upset anyone. A ticket clerk for the railway, it is obvious that he will remain as he is for the rest of his life. Mrs Johnson we know little about, except that she takes delight in organising other people's lives, and when Mr Polly decides to get married, she is not at all concerned about him, but selfishly upset because it means she might lose money. She is a selfish, sharp and unpleasant woman, though capable of being kind to Mr Polly as long as he does what she wants.

Miriam

Miriam is a dark, thin girl, with a serious expression. She has a 'rather lean and insufficient body', and is 'flat chested'. There is no particular reason for Mr Polly choosing to marry her rather than one of her sisters, and, after the marriage, she 'developed a meagre and serious quality of her own, and went about with knitted brows pursuing some ideal of ''aving everything right'. Wells also says that she 'combined earnestness of spirit with great practical incapacity'; she is always tidying up, but somehow things never get tidy. She cooks because she has to, and does it very badly. Almost her first reaction on seeing the supposedly drowned

Mr Polly is to say, ''Ow we'll pay back the Insurance now, I *don't* know', and this shows how little she has ever loved her husband.

It has been said that Wells is unsympathetic and unfair to Miriam, letting us see her only through the eyes of Mr Polly, and never giving us her view of the situation. It is true that she is not an evil woman, but then she does not get treated as such. She receives more from Mr Polly than ever she gave him, and in her own way she is as happy in her tea-shop as Mr Polly is at the end of the novel; there is no question of Wells punishing her. The truth is that Miriam is a sour and not very attractive woman whose true nature was hidden from Mr Polly by the jollity that surrounded her in the Larkins household. They are totally unsuited for each other, and she never tries to understand Mr Polly, dismissing his moods as 'Tantrums!' and ceasing to listen to him as soon as they are married.

The landlady

We are told very little about the landlady, and most of what we are told can be found in two passages. She is 'agreeable, motherly, comfortable', and a good cook. Wells describes her in the following terms:

> Many people would have called her a fat woman, but Mr Polly's innate sense of epithet told him from the outset that plump was the word. [Wells later tells us that she does become fat in later years]. She had shapely brows and a straight, well-shaped nose, kind lines and contentment about her mouth, and beneath it the jolly chins clustered like chubby little cherubim about the feet of an Assumption-ing Madonna. Her plumpness was firm and pink and wholesome, and her hands, dimpled at every joint, were clasped in front of her; she seemed, as it were, to embrace herself with infinite confidence and kindliness, as one who knew herself good in substance, good in essence, and would show her gratitude to God by that ready acceptance of all that He had given her. Her head was a little on one side, not much, but just enough to speak of trustfulness, and rob her of the stiff effect of self-reliance.

Perhaps most necessary of all for Mr Polly, she is a good listener, and in need of help. They are friends at first sight, and she is everything that Miriam is not.

Uncle Jim

Uncle Jim is given a big build-up before he appears, and when we do see him, it is not an anti-climax:

> Uncle Jim was certainly not a handsome person. He was short, shorter

than Mr Polly, with long arms and lean, big hands; a thin and wiry neck stuck out of his grey flannel shirt, and supported a big head that had something of the snake in the convergent lines of its broad, knobby brow, meanly proportioned face, and pointed chin. His almost toothless mouth seemed a cavern in the twilight. Some accident had left him with one small and active, and one large and expressionless reddish eye, and wisps of straight hair strayed from under the blue cricket cap he had pulled down obliquely over the latter.

Uncle Jim is a cruel and vicious criminal; he terrorises his aunt and takes money from her, terrorises her employees, and is corrupting the landlady's young granddaughter by teaching her to swear and spit. However, as the chapter progresses and Mr Polly gets the better of him, he increasingly becomes a comic figure, a stupid, blundering oaf who thoroughly deserves to be drowned. Although Mr Polly can find it in him to feel a little sympathy for Jim, the reader feels none. His role in the book is to provide a reason for Mr Polly's change of character, and to make Wells's vision of the countryside a little more credible.

The minor characters

Very few of these play a significant part in the plot, but the little pen-sketches that Wells gives are often highly comic, and enrich the novel.

Platt is 'white-faced and dark, and disposed to undertones and mystery, and a curiosity about society'. He is also an apprentice at Port Burdock, but becomes 'a tiresome companion' when Parsons leaves the store.

Morrison is an 'improver' in the Port Burdock shop, and profoundly religious. He lacks 'Joy de Vive'.

Mr Garvace is senior partner and managing director of the Port Burdock Bazaar, and is known as 'little Fluffums'. He is assaulted by Parsons.

Mr Polly's father was an 'irritable stranger', but when we read that he was 'a weakly wilful being, struggling to get obdurate things round impossible corners' we can see that he is, in a small way, a symbol of all those people like Mr Polly who feel themselves powerless to influence events.

Podger is the undertaker who buries Mr Polly's father.

Mr and Mrs Rymer own and run a butcher's shop in Easewood.

Aunt Larkins is Miriam's mother. She is a fat, freckle-faced woman who makes up her mind that Mr Polly will marry one of her daughters. She is jolly, but disorganised, and it is not clear whether she actually believes her daughters are as marvellous as she says, or merely says so to trap Mr Polly.

Annie Larkins is Miriam's sister, a large, loud, and clumsy girl, although apparently good-natured.

Minnie Larkins is Miriam's other sister.

Uncle Pentstemon is a mean old man with a hollow tooth and arthritis. He is 'very much bent', 'an aged rather than venerable figure', and like 'a fragment from the ruder agricultural past of our race, like a lump of soil among things of paper'. He has no tact and none of the social graces, is scathingly rude about the Larkins family, whom he looks down on because they go out to work, and prides himself on his generosity, when his wedding present to Mr Polly is an old broken tea-caddy for which he has no further use. He is one of the best examples of Wells's skill in creating minor comic characters.

May Punt is a small woman with a son who eats too much, called Willy.

Ascough is head of the boot shop in Clapham.

Christabel, the schoolgirl, is red-haired and good-looking. She is at boarding school because her parents are working abroad, and she is interested and charmed by Mr Polly. She shows how much of an incurable romantic Mr Polly is, and her betrayal of him sends him into the arms of Miriam.

Mr Voules is a Larkins uncle, a 'fat, short, red-faced man', rather pleased with himself and very much in command of the situation at the wedding. He is efficient, but more interested in the party after the wedding than he is in Mr Polly, and he likes to take charge of situations.

Wintershed, Clamp, Gambell and Carter are shopkeepers in Fishbourne.

Rumbold is a dour and taciturn neighbour of Mr Polly's who runs a china shop. He has an argument with Mr Polly, and is on the edge of bankruptcy.

Hinks is a saddler, and a 'sporting man' who is big and argumentative, wears loud clothes, and threatens Mr Polly for talking about him behind his back.

Chuffles is a grocer in Fishbourne and 'totally uninteresting'.

Tonks is another grocer, and very pious.

Boomer is a wine merchant in Fishbourne. He and **Tashingford** the chemist pride themselves on being better than the other shopkeepers.

Rusper is a serious-faced man with a speech defect. He is an ironmonger, and a neighbour of Mr Polly's. He reads a lot, though not like Mr Polly, and for a short while they are friendly, though they later have a feud. Rusper also has an amazing, egg-shaped bald head.

Taplow is a policeman in Fishbourne.

The old lady lives with Rumbold. She quite enjoys the fire and being rescued, and is another superbly comic character. She is Rumbold's mother-in-law.

Lady Bargrave is a titled lady who lives in Fishbourne, and pays for accommodation for those who have lost their homes in the fire.

The landlady's granddaughter is falling under the influence of Jim, although she eventually comes to like Mr Polly. She has 'black hair and brown legs and a buff short frock and very intelligent eyes'.

Warspite is 'a literary man' who suffers from insomnia; he finds Mr Polly hiding from Jim.

Blake is the village policeman.

The narrator

We know little about the narrator in *The History of Mr Polly*, although he is a strong presence in the book. We assume that he is H. G. Wells, but it is wise not to take this assumption too far. For the purposes of a book, and when it suits him, an author can take on an imagined character, as fictional as any in the book.

The narrator is a benign and sympathetic personality. Occasionally he steps into the novel, as when he lectures us on Education, or tells us about the views of Sidney Webb. He guides our view of the various characters, and tells us specifically what to think on some occasions, usually where it concerns Mr Polly. There are the narrator's remarks on Mr Polly's arson, telling us that we should not be bothered about it, and minor comments such as, 'For a time our Mr Polly has figured heroic. Now comes the fall again.' He restricts us largely to Mr Polly's viewpoint, not telling us, for example, what conversations and discussions take place in the Larkins household when Mr Polly leaves, and he tells the story with a calm air of authority. He stands sufficiently outside of the story to be able to tell us with some surprise that Mr Polly does not like Dickens, implying that the narrator does. Above all, the narrator is the teller of the story, and he does not give us the impression that he is also the creator; we do not feel that he could change or alter events at a mere whim, and in this sense the narrator acts more like a historian, a recorder of facts, than a novelist.

Style

An author's style is the way he writes; it can include such matters as his choice of words, the length of his sentences, the metaphors and similes he uses, his use of dialogue, and the frequency and style of his descriptive passages.

Wells's style in *The History of Mr Polly* is simple, straightforward, and unadorned. Occasionally it is careless; the most famous example is when he writes 'The house was never clean nor tidy', where 'or' should be used in place of 'nor', but bad grammar like this is rare in the novel. Wells can bend the rules, however, especially in his use of capitals to emphasise a word or phrase; there is no grammatical reason for the shop assistant's nouns being in capitals when he says Mr Polly has 'no Zest! no Vim!', except Wells's desire to suggest the words are spoken with explosive force, and when Mrs Johnson talks about 'A Great Crowd' coming to the funeral, the capitals are used to suggest that this is a well-known phrase.

Some aspects of Wells's style have caused annoyance to critics; one of these is Mr Polly's odd or unusual use of words. At crucial moments in the book, like the fire or the first fight with Uncle Jim, the Pollyisms disappear. Wells's habit of stopping the action for a personal comment ('I remember seeing a picture of Education . . .') is something he may have inherited from earlier novelists, and the action is further held up by long passages of detailed description of rooms or places. It has been said that these are unreal, because in real life we are not able to take in immediately as much as we are told by Wells. However, the idea that the novel is made more unreal because of these features needs to be treated with caution. Very few novels are real, in the sense of being like real life, and we accept a degree of artificiality in any work of fiction. Even if we do lose a little reality by having an intrusive narrator, we gain something as well, namely a dual vision of Mr Polly. The narrator, because he is an independent figure with an existence of his own, can take an outside view of Mr Polly, and put our view of him into perspective. For much of the novel we walk side by side with Mr Polly, but the independent narrator can move away and give us a more objective view.

Wells's style is seen at its best in two types of writing: the descriptive passages, and the action scenes. The first major descriptive passage comes when Mr Polly is rambling the countryside with Parsons and Platt (it starts with 'There is no country-side like the English country-side . . .'), and there are further examples at the end of the book. The language of these passages is simple yet evocative, the atmosphere of spring and sunshine overwhelming, and the sheer joy that the author takes in the countryside comes over with great strength. You should notice, however, that there are other, less happy, passages of description, such as Mr Polly's train journey to Easewood; though they do not deal in beauty, these are no less effective, and again illustrate Wells's ability to draw simple and vivid pictures of his surroundings.

The scenes of action, such as the fights with Uncle Jim and the fire, are equally effective. The action moves very fast, often breathlessly so, but Wells never loses sight of the people involved in the incidents which he describes; it is because the participants see the significance of what is happening that we share their view, and become involved ourselves.

The mock heroic style

Indigestion in an insignificant member of society is not going to shake the world to its roots. Wells describes Mr Polly's stomach troubles in terms of a vast war or revolution, and humour is the result. This technique, describing a trivial incident in terms that are far too glorious for it, is a well-known literary device, and is called the mock heroic style. He uses it again in his descriptions of the battles with Uncle Jim, as when he writes 'Certain compensating qualities of the very greatest military value were appearing in Mr Polly, even as he ran.' There are times also in the description of the great Fishbourne fire when the reader feels as if the whole world is alight. On the other hand, Wells is very careful that we never lose sight of how trivial these events really are, for the humour rests in the incompatibility of the inflated descriptions with reality.

Irony

Irony occurs when a line or word has an apparent or superficial meaning, but carries also within it another meaning, often contradictory to the surface meaning. Irony is therefore double-meaning; sarcasm is a very simple form of irony, as when someone says 'You *are* intelligent!' to someone who has just made a very stupid remark; in effect, the speaker is saying, 'You are not intelligent.' There are very many types of irony.

There is a great deal of irony in *The History of Mr Polly*, and it is one of Wells's main comic techniques. There are too many examples to list here, but you should be able to spot many of them yourself. Thus when Miriam says 'But there seems to be no pleasing some people' after Mr Polly's meal in Chapter 1, we know and can see that Mr Polly has every reason not to be pleased. Wells's comment on Mrs Johnson that 'She made dying seem almost agreeable' is heavily ironical; for Mrs Johnson, dying is agreeable, as long as it is not her own death. It is simply an excuse to spend someone else's money on a party. 'Always glad of good wishes', says Mr Polly to Harold Johnson, knowing full well that Johnson has just been making the most gloomy prophecies about Mr Polly's marriage. When Rusper and Polly have a fight, 'At any cost they perceived they must not become ridiculous'; but we can see that they have already made themselves look very ridiculous. Then there is Rusper reading pamphlets which talk about vast sums of money, when he is short of two pennies to rub together, as the saying goes.

Dialogue

Another of Wells's skills is dialogue, or conversation between characters. His attempts to imitate accents are sometimes clumsy (for instance,

Elfrid for Alfred), but each of his characters seems to acquire his or her own style of speech, from Aunt Larkins's flustered and breathless jollity to the measured and ever so sensible tones of Harold Johnson. If you open your copy of *The History of Mr Polly* at any page where someone is speaking, and do not look to see who it is, you will be surprised at how easily you can recognise the speaker. It is almost as if Wells can give a form of signature tune to each character; sometimes a character becomes tied to one particular phrase, like Mr Voules and his ''Ave some more 'am?'.

Wells was very well read, and occasionally his learning creeps into the novel, as when he mentions 'Laocoon' and 'Obi'. However, his style is generally not difficult, and reads easily. He is not a great user of the English language, like Dickens, or even Shakespeare, but his style is effective, and occasionally powerful.

Part 4

Hints for study

Points to select for detailed study

Part 3 covers most of the points you are liable to find asked in any examination on *The History of Mr Polly*, and the areas outlined in that section are those on which you should undertake detailed study. However, there are certain passages which, because they say a great deal or illustrate some point of major importance, you should study in detail. Your examination may be the type that has a context question in it, that is an extract from the book, on which you are asked to comment or answer questions. Some of the passages selected below are quite likely to be set as context questions, but you should not rely on this at all; a context question may be drawn from any area of the text, and there is even a chance that your examiner, if he has read these Notes, may steer clear of passages recommended in it! However, these passages, if studied in detail and understood, will tell you a great deal about the novel.

You should read the opening of a work of literature very carefully and you should also be very familiar with the first paragraph of section 2, the description of Mr Polly.

Chapter 2 is worthy of close study, especially the fight in the window; it is a good example of Wells's comic writing, with undertones of tragedy, and the incident is a major turning-point in Mr Polly's life.

The opening of Chapter 4, which gives us Mr Polly's thoughts about his father, shows Wells in more serious mood.

Section 3 of this chapter should also be read with care, because it introduces the Larkinses and Uncle Pentstemon. Section 5 should be studied in detail, for what it tells us about Wells's skill in set-piece comic scenes and dialogue.

Another turning-point is Mr Polly's meeting with Christabel, the schoolgirl, in Chapter 5, and this should be studied in detail. Section 2 of Chapter 6, the proposal to Miriam, is of obvious significance, as is section 5, the marriage itself. Section 6 is another set-piece comic scene, with skilful portrayal of dialogue. The fight with Rusper in section 6 of Chapter 7 is Wells's tragicomedy at its best.

The description of the Fishbourne fire and the first fight with Uncle Jim are two of the most memorable passages in the book, and should be studied in close detail. The first section of Chapter 9 is vital, as it shows us Mr Polly breaking free, and the second section of this chapter, section

3 of the last chapter, and section 4 of the first chapter provide the best examples of Wells's descriptive style, as it concerns nature. The last chapter itself needs to be thoroughly understood, as it is a conclusion for the whole book.

It is no bad idea to mark these passages in your book, together with any lengthy passages that have been quoted in these Notes, such as the descriptions of the landlady and Uncle Jim.

Quotations

Any effective examination answer will require you to quote from the book to back up or illustrate the points you make. If you are allowed to take a copy of the book into the examination you should mark clearly those passages from which you think you might wish to quote; but be very careful. Students taking examinations that allow them to use the book often find either that their answers consist almost wholly of quotation, or that they spend far too much time searching through the book to find the lines they want. You should never need to quote more than a few lines, and those only when they are relevant. After all, an examiner can read Wells's lines simply by picking up his own copy of the book, and what interests him is your understanding and knowledge of the book.

A good way of proceeding is to make a list, on a sheet of paper, of all the lines quoted in the course of these Notes, and then add to it the lines given below. This list will be a long one. If you are allowed to take a copy of the book into your examination, you should then mark these quotations in your book. If not, you should select about thirty lines, or possibly forty, which cover the main areas of importance, and learn them. Remember to learn them exactly, even down to the punctuation. You will lose a lot of marks for incorrect quotation, for the same reason that a lawyer would be heavily punished for falsifying evidence.

Chapter 1

'Nothing felt right' and 'I'm pretty near sick of everything'. These lines sum up Mr Polly's mood.

'I 'aven't patience.' This sums up Miriam!

'Fishbourne seemed a very jolly little place to Mr Polly that afternoon.' This looks forward to Mr Polly's future.

Chapter 3

'It was after Canterbury that the universe became really disagreeable to Mr Polly.' This illustrates a turning-point.

'Might do worse,' said Johnson, 'than put it into a small shop.' This line shows where Mr Polly got the idea of a small shop from.

'Hen-witted gigglers' shows Mr Polly's first, and correct, judgement of those at the funeral party.

Chapter 5

'Every road, he remarked as freshly as though he had never observed it before, was bordered by inflexible palings or iron fences or severely disciplined hedges.' This is a symbol of the way Mr Polly is constrained and held in in his life.

'I'm not a bit tidy, I know, but I do like to 'ave a go in at things now and then.' Miriam sums herself up.

Chapter 6

'It was almost irresistibly fascinating to think how immensely a few words from him would excite and revolutionize Minnie.' This suggests that a proposal from Mr Polly is likely to be given for all the wrong reasons.

'For the life of him Mr Polly could not tell whether he was full of tender anticipations or regretful panic' and 'He had a curious feeling that it would be very satisfying to marry and have a wife—only somehow he wished it wasn't Miriam.'

'He tried to assure himself that he was acting upon his own forceful initiative, but at the back of his mind was the completest realization of his powerlessness to resist the gigantic social forces he had set in motion.' This powerlessness is a major theme of the book.

Chapter 7

'It was a reluctant little shop from the beginning.' The following extract sums up both Mr Polly's life and his state of mind up to the time of the fire:

> Suddenly, one day it came to him—forgetful of those books and all he had lived and seen through them—that he had been in his shop for exactly fifteen years, that he would soon be forty, and that his life during that time had not been worth living, that it had been in apathetic and feebly hostile and critical company, ugly in detail and mean in scope, and that it had brought him at last to an outlook utterly hopeless and grey.

Chapter 8

'And it seemed to him now that life had never begun for him, never! It was as if his soul had been cramped and his eyes bandaged from the hour of his birth.'

Chapter 9

The following extract shows us the re-birth of Mr Polly:

Life had never been so clear to him before. It had always been a confused, entertaining spectacle. He had responded to this impulse and that, seeking agreeable and entertaining things, evading difficult and painful things. Such is the way of those who grow up to a life that has neither danger nor honour in its texture. He had been muddled and wrapped about and entangled, like a creature born in the jungle who has never seen sea or sky. Now he had come out of it suddenly into a great exposed place. It was as if God and Heaven waited over him, and all the earth was expectation.

'A novelist should present characters, not vivisect them publicly...' This is an interesting comment on Wells's technique of characterisation.

Effective arrangement of material

Examination questions tend to be of two types, either factual or discursive. The factual question simply tests your knowledge of the book, but the discursive question asks you to use your knowledge to develop an argument and comment on the book. This section is largely concerned with the discursive answer.

There are a number of general points which apply to all discursive answers.

Relevance and answering the question

Very few questions, if any, will ask you to pour out everything you know about *The History of Mr Polly*; usually you will be asked to select details on a particular point or area of interest. Only details that are relevant to the particular question asked will gain you marks. If you know a lot about the book, there is a tremendous temptation to show the examiner this, and ignore the specific question you have been asked. If we take as an example a question like 'Is society to blame for Mr Polly's unhappiness, or Mr Polly himself?', then details like Wells's skill as a descriptive writer, Mr Polly's misuse of language, and the question of whether or not we lose interest in the narrator's digressions are of no use at all for answering this question. You must also make sure you understand the title correctly, and so know which area you are being asked about. Do not rush into an answer before you have fully studied the question.

Developing an argument

In a question like the one above, there are two different points of view. Always make sure that you cover both sides of the question in a case like this; you might believe that it is Mr Polly's fault, but it is also possible to take the other view, and the examiner will not be convinced or impressed with your answer unless you tell him not only why your view is right, but why the other view is wrong. You must also avoid not coming to any conclusion; an answer which ends with a sentence like 'It is possible to hold both points of view, and I do not know which is the better' is a disaster. It suggests that all you know about *The History of Mr Polly* is what other people have told you, and that you have no opinions of your own.

Planning an answer

With an evenly-balanced question like the one above, how do you know which view to support? The answer is that there will be evidence to support both points of view, and you must argue the one for which you can muster the most evidence. The only way you will be able to decide which one this is is to plan the essay in note form before you write it; this way, you will see for which point of view you have most evidence, and thus avoid the awful situation where you start arguing one side of a case, and half-way through the answer find that you have convinced yourself that the other side is the right one. Planning not only lets you organise your information to best advantage, but gives you a few extra minutes to think out the implications of the question.

There are four stages in the writing of a good plan.

(i) *Note down rough ideas.* After you have looked at the question, put down on paper, in note form, the ideas which you think you might be able to use, such as:

Society educates Mr Polly badly
Mr Polly is weak-willed and a dreamer
Mr Polly strongly influenced by other people
Mr Polly forced into job he hates
Job itself difficult to do well
Other shopkeepers can be successful
Many shopkeepers as miserable as Mr Polly

Extract from Sidney Webb's works suggest society at fault
Mr Polly can alter things, change his unhappiness
Suggestion that all lower middle class is miserable
Countryside more attractive than town
Other people very unsympathetic towards Mr Polly
Mr Polly upsets other people, and is not easy to get on with

(ii) *Organise ideas into paragraphs.* Take your rough ideas and divide them up into separate paragraphs, at the same time cutting out irrelevant or unnecessary ideas. Can you see which ideas have been left out?

1. Society educates Mr Polly badly
   Job itself difficult to do well, Polly forced into job he hates
   Extract from Sidney Webb's works suggests society is at fault
   Many shopkeepers as miserable as Mr Polly
   Suggestion all lower middle class as miserable as Mr Polly

2. Other people unsympathetic towards Mr Polly
   Mr Polly strongly influenced by other people

3. Mr Polly is weak-willed and a dreamer
   He upsets other people, and is not easy to get on with
   Other shopkeepers can do well

4. Mr Polly can alter things, change his unhappiness

Having established what the content of our paragraphs is going to be, the next stage is to decide the order in which these paragraphs should stand in the essay.

(iii) *Put paragraphs in order and write conclusion.* To put the paragraphs in the right order, it is necessary to know what your conclusion is going to be, because you should always finish your essay with the strongest arguments in your favour. Yet in this answer we have a problem; the arguments on both sides seem to be of roughly equal strength. Our conclusion is therefore not likely to be wholly in favour of it being society's fault or Mr Polly's, but a mixture or compromise. We might say that society contributes a lot to Mr Polly's unhappiness, but that on balance it is more his fault, because the ending of the novel shows us that it is always within the power of the individual to alter his state of mind and his position in life. For this conclusion, the paragraphs are already in a satisfactory order, and so do not need to be changed.

(iv) *Write topic sentences and find evidence.* The final stage before you actually write your answer is to make up topic sentences for each paragraph. A topic sentence is the first sentence in a paragraph, and it states in a few words what the subject or the point of that paragraph is. It is useful because it gives the reader an immediate grasp of what you are saying, and because you can use your topic sentences to check whether or not you are answering the question. As it sums up the message of the paragraph, you know that if this topic sentence is not directly relevant to the title, you need to re-write the paragraph and make it more relevant.

The only other thing you should do is choose quotations and examples to back up the points you wish to make, and write these in on the plan. Remember that if you cannot refer to a specific place or line in the novel as evidence for what you are saying, then there is a strong chance that you are on the wrong track, and inventing something that Wells did not say or mean.

This process of planning is a long one, but with practice, it becomes automatic, and need only take up five minutes or so of your time in an examination. These are the most important five minutes of the whole examination.

The actual answer written from this plan might look like the specimen below; but remember it is only one possible answer, and not necessarily the only one that is right.

You will always find that extra ideas creep into your answer as you are writing it; you should not worry about this, but just make sure the ideas are as relevant as the ones in the plan, and put them into the answer in the best place.

Specimen questions and answers

Is society to blame for Mr Polly's unhappiness, or Mr Polly himself?

Mr Polly says at the start of *The History of Mr Polly*, 'I'm pretty near sick of everything', and society undoubtedly must take some of the blame for his unhappiness. A good education might have taught him more about himself, or at least given him the knowledge to run his business more efficiently, but society has failed to provide this. Mr Polly is made to do a job he dislikes, through no choice of his own, and a job in which it is difficult to feel happy, because it is badly paid and offers miserable conditions. Wells's references to the works of Sidney Webb suggest that people like Mr Polly have no control over their lives, and are held powerless in the grip of social forces that they cannot understand. Finally, nearly all the shopkeepers and members of the lower middle class that we see are unhappy, or at least not leading very fruitful or satisfying lives. All these points tend to suggest that society is to blame for Mr Polly's misery.

Other members of society are also to blame for this misery. His father puts him into an unsatisfying job. Harold Johnson gives him bad advice about opening a shop, and he is trapped into an awful marriage by Mrs Larkins and Miriam. Very few people are kind to him, at least until after the fire and at the Potwell Inn, and not all of this is Mr Polly's fault.

On the other hand, Mr Polly brings a lot of trouble down on himself. He is weak-willed and a romantic dreamer, and gets himself dismissed from a number of jobs because of this. His troubled romance with the schoolgirl is his own fault, because he insists on seeing the girl as an ideal figure, and not as what she really is. He has many annoying habits, and cannot be easy to make friends with. The failure of his shop must be at least partly his fault, because not all shopkeepers are failures: Mr and Mrs Rymer, who run a pork butcher's shop in Easewood, seem to make a good living out of it. Some things society cannot be blamed for; his indigestion makes him miserable, but it is not given him by society.

It might therefore seem that society and Mr Polly are equally to blame for Mr Polly's unhappiness. However, it is possible to argue that Mr Polly is more at fault, because he could always have 'cleared out' and changed his situation, and it is only his own indecision and cowardice that stop him from doing so. The answer is therefore that society helps create Mr Polly's misery, but Mr Polly is responsible for prolonging it by his failure to realise that 'If the world does not please you, *you can change it.*'

What are the main features of Wells's style in *The History of Mr Polly*?

Wells's style is simple and unadorned. It can also be careless, as when he writes, 'The house was never clean nor tidy', where 'or' should be used in place of 'nor'; but this is not common in the novel. His use of capital letters is not always grammatically correct, as when he has Mrs Johnson talk about 'A Great Crowd' coming to the funeral, but his free use of capitals in dialogue can be effective in giving emphasis to certain words and phrases.

One stylistic feature in *The History of Mr Polly* that has received adverse criticism is Mr Polly's mispronunciation and misunderstanding of words. If this is a joke, it can be argued that Wells allows it to go on for too long, and that words like 'Delphicums' and 'Vorocious' simply confuse the reader without amusing him. Similarly, Wells's phonetic spelling of words ('Drorback' for 'drawback', 'bolls' for 'bottles') can be confusing, although it can also help convey the atmosphere of a scene, or details of a speaker's character. Another complaint often levelled against Wells's style in this novel is that some of the detailed descriptions hold up the flow of the story without making any worthwhile contribution to the book as a whole, as, for instance, when Wells describes Mr Polly's train journey. Wells's habit of stopping the action for a personal comment by the narrator ('I remember seeing a picture of Education ...') can be criticised for the same reasons.

Wells's style is seen at its best in two types of writing: the descriptive passages, and the action scenes. The success of some of the descriptive passages outweighs any tendency they might have to hold up the story. They are simple but evocative, as when Wells is describing Mr Polly's rambling on his way to the Potwell Inn:

> For a time the wanderer stopped and stood still, and even the thin whistle died away from his lips as he watched a water-vole run to and fro upon a little headland across the stream. The vole plopped into the water, and swam and dived, and only when the last ring of its disturbance had vanished did Mr Polly resume his thoughtful course to nowhere in particular.

There is no great wealth of detail here, but some very carefully chosen images, and accurate observation of natural detail. The action scenes, in particular the descriptions of the Fishbourne fire and the fight between Uncle Jim and Mr Polly, are triumphs. They are both frightening and comic, and combine fast-moving action with character observation. To use Wells's own words, they are full of 'Zest!' and 'Vim!', and reveal the absolute delight Wells has in scenes of noise, tumult, and confusion.

Wells also makes skilful use of the mock heroic style, where insignificant events are described as if they were of the utmost importance. Thus Mr Polly's upset stomach is written about in terms that could be equally well applied to an account or description of the French Revolution, and the fight between Uncle Jim and Mr Polly described in a manner that would not disgrace a description of a famous general's campaigns: 'Certain compensating qualities of the very greatest military value were appearing in Mr Polly, even as he ran.' Wells creates much warm-hearted comedy by his use of this technique.

Although Wells's style is simple, it can achieve some complex effects, the main one of which is the successful blending of comic and semi-tragic moods. We laugh a lot in the novel, but are never allowed to forget that the problems faced by the characters in it are serious, and worthy of our concern. The weaknesses of Wells's style, such as the occasional careless error, informal punctuation, or interruptions to the narrative, are outweighed by its strengths: simplicity, humour, and a shrewd eye for the vital details that breathe warmth and life into a scene or a character.

Discuss the contribution made by Uncle Jim to *The History of Mr Polly*.

Uncle Jim is one of the most memorable characters in *The History of Mr Polly*. Although he only appears at a relatively late stage in the story, he makes a useful contribution to the success of the novel.

Uncle Jim is a violent, ignorant criminal, and one of his main functions is to bring a touch of the real world into the book. The Potwell

Inn is an idyllic environment for Mr Polly, and one of the criticisms
levelled at *The History of Mr Polly* is that it paints an unrealistically
beautiful portrait of the countryside, one that the reader finds difficult to
believe. Into this haven of peace and contentment comes Uncle Jim, a
bull-like figure intent on destroying all Mr Polly has sought after and
achieved. His arrival shows us that misery and persecution occur in the
countryside as well as in the towns, and that moving to a rural retreat is
not on its own an answer to life's problems.

Uncle Jim also performs a vital role in that he provides a final test for
Mr Polly; the conflict between the two brings out the best in Mr Polly,
and forces him to prove himself. Mr Polly is too ordinary to be classed as
a great hero, but his decision to stand and face Uncle Jim raises him in
the eyes of the reader, and shows us how much he has learnt in his wand-
erings. When Wells writes of Mr Polly that 'he turned his face towards
the Potwell Inn', meaning that he decided to stand and fight Uncle Jim,
it is his greatest moment. The decision to stay and its outcome are what
lead directly to Mr Polly being able to live out the rest of his days in
peace and contentment, and so prove one of the novel's main statements, that, 'If the world does not please you, *you can change it.*'

Uncle Jim shows us that cruelty and harshness exist in town as well as
country, and is the means whereby Mr Polly proves himself, but it is
largely as a comic figure that he is remembered. His attempts to defeat
Mr Polly at the Potwell Inn provide material for some of the most
successful comic passages in the novel, uproariously funny sequences in
which we see Uncle Jim first confused, then humiliated, and finally
driven off.

Uncle Jim also gives the novel added variety. Many of the figures in
The History of Mr Polly are drawn from the same social class as Mr Polly
himself, whereas Uncle Jim is a member of the criminal classes, and as
such adds a new dimension to the book. He is also vital to the plot; if it
were not for him being mistakenly identified as Mr Polly, Miriam might
not have been able to set up in business with the insurance money, and
hence Mr Polly's happiness at the Potwell Inn placed in jeopardy.

Uncle Jim contributes greatly to the success of *The History of Mr
Polly*. He adds to the novel's comedy and its tension, and provides both
variety and an opportunity for Mr Polly to prove himself as a man in
command of his own destiny.

'The real hero of *The History of Mr Polly* is human nature.' Discuss.

The hero of a novel is its central figure, a character who invites the
respect and admiration of the reader. In some respects, this definition
applies to Mr Polly. He is the central figure in the novel, which bears his
name in its title, and the reader is asked by Wells to sympathise with his

problems, share them, and feel pleasure at the eventual peace and contentment that he achieves. He also has some of the characteristics that are traditionally associated with heroes: a trace of bravery in his fights with Uncle Jim, and his rescue of the old lady in the Fishbourne fire, and a generous heart, as shown by his concern for Miriam.

However, he also has a number of features which are not heroic. He is short and plump, and we rarely hear of a traditional hero having chronic indigestion. He is a comic figure, and although we sometimes laugh with him, we often laugh at him and his limitations. The examples of his heroism are matched by those of his cowardice. He spends as much time running away from Uncle Jim as he does fighting him, and he cannot carry through the relatively simple act of killing himself. He can be a truculent and argumentative figure at times, and one who brings trouble down upon himself, as in his fight with Rusper.

If Mr Polly cannot be automatically called the hero of the novel, it is equally difficult to apply this term to 'human nature'. For us to be able to do so, it would have to be proved that the novel was about humanity in general, and that what it showed was that all humanity was worthy of our respect and admiration. This is not the case; the majority of characters in the novel could in no sense be classified as heroic. We neither respect nor admire characters such as Miriam (a mean, unsympathetic woman), Uncle Jim (a violent criminal), and Harold Johnson (an empty nonentity), and the only one who might qualify is the landlady. There are certainly characters in the novel who do have admirable features and reflect credit on human nature, but there are an equal if not larger number who do not.

The answer is that the true hero of the novel is a combination of Mr Polly *and* human nature. Mr Polly is not a perfect being, nor a perfect hero, but this is his great strength; he shows us that even flawed human-beings can find the strength to challenge life and take their destiny into their own hands; even cowards like Mr Polly can find at least a trace of bravery in themselves, if the need is strong enough. The real hero of the novel is not Mr Polly, nor all humanity, but that group of people represented by Mr Polly, the 'little men' whose lives are a desperate struggle to retain dignity and self-respect. Wells is too honest to say that all humanity is worthy of our respect and admiration, but generous enough to admit that at least some are, even if they too have their faults and weaknesses.

Further essay questions

1. Write on the autobiographical elements in *The History of Mr Polly*.
2. What would you say are the main weaknesses of *The History of Mr Polly*?

3. 'The conflict in this novel is not between Mr Polly and an outside force like society, but is all within himself.' Discuss, saying whether you think this is a true statement or not.
4. How true is it to say that Mr Polly is the only character in the novel drawn in any depth?
5. How does Wells achieve his comic effects?
6. Is Wells unfair to Miriam?
7. 'The narrator appears too often.' How much do you think the narrator's digressions and lectures, and the lengthy descriptions of setting, slow up and weaken the novel?
8. *The History of Mr Polly* has been described as a tragicomedy. How much of it do you think is tragic, and how much comic?
9. How accurate is it to describe Mr Polly as 'a coward and a dreamer'?
10. Discuss the contribution made to the novel by the following: Mr Polly's father; Aunt Larkins; Uncle Pentstemon.
11. Analyse in detail the technique and style of the meal that takes place after the funeral of Mr Polly's father.
12. Why does Mr Polly marry Miriam?
13. Discuss Wells's treatment of: education; the church.
14. What are the things that Mr Polly most wants out of life, and why cannot he get them?
15. Discuss some of the methods by which Wells tries to create the impression that this is a true-to-life story.
16. Discuss the treatment of the countryside in the novel.
17. Would you describe *The History of Mr Polly* as 'escapist'?
18. What is there in Mr Polly to make us feel sympathy towards him?
19. What is Uncle Jim's function in the novel?
20. Discuss Wells's use of irony and the mock heroic style.
21. Do you agree with the statement that 'the landlady is the most interesting character in the novel'?
22. Why is Mr Polly so happy at the Potwell Inn?
23. Wells often wrote in a hurry, and rarely revised what he wrote. What evidence of this is there in *The History of Mr Polly*?
24. What would you say is the main theme of the novel, and why do you think it dominates?
25. To what extent is Mr Polly a representative figure?
26. How successful is Wells in creating minor characters?
27. To what extent is the theme of *The History of Mr Polly* the problems of middle age?
28. How limited is the range of character in the novel, and how much is this a weakness?
29. Is Wells biased against women?
30. How true is it to say that what Wells always shows us is the weakness of his characters, and not the strength?